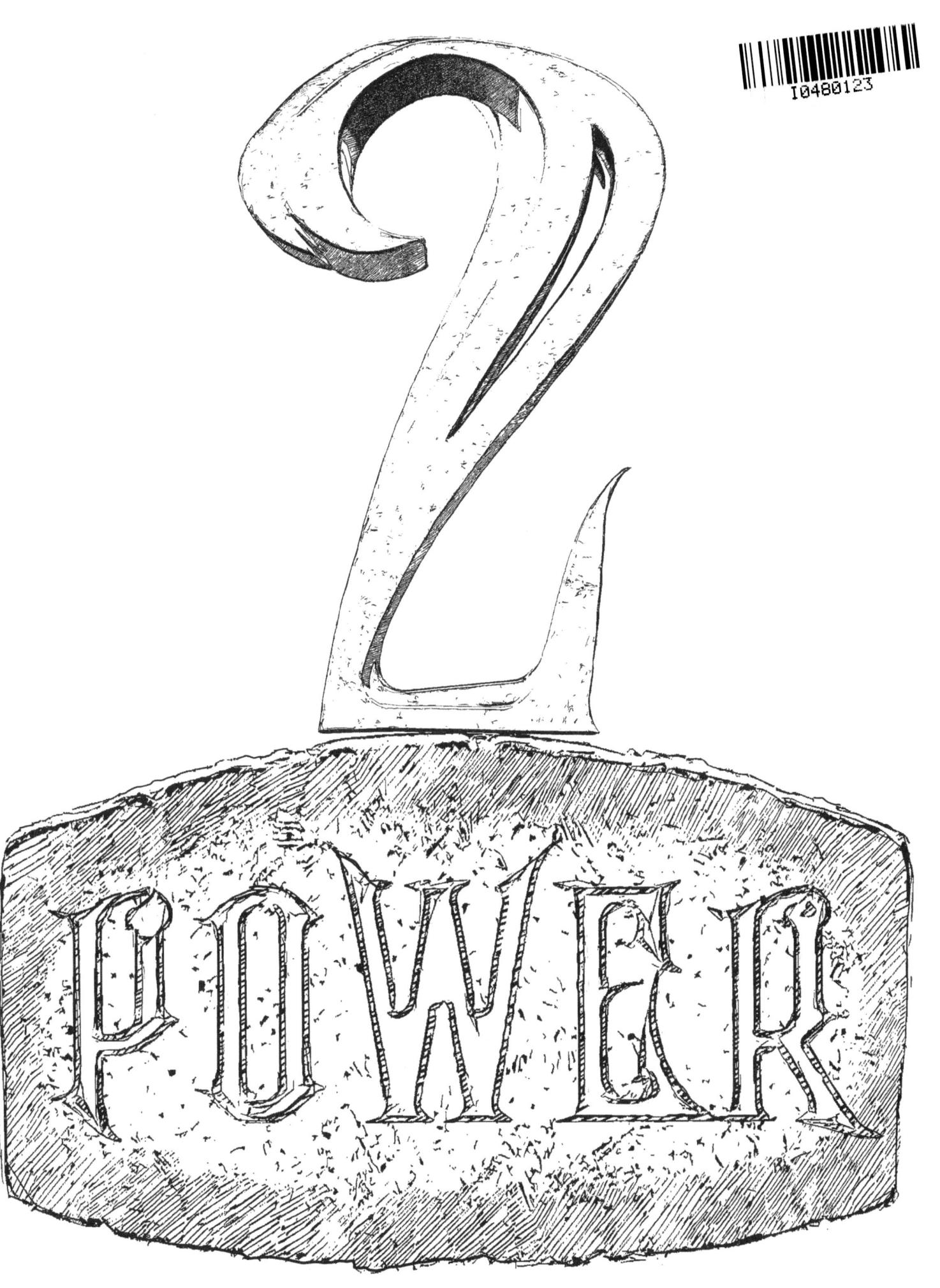

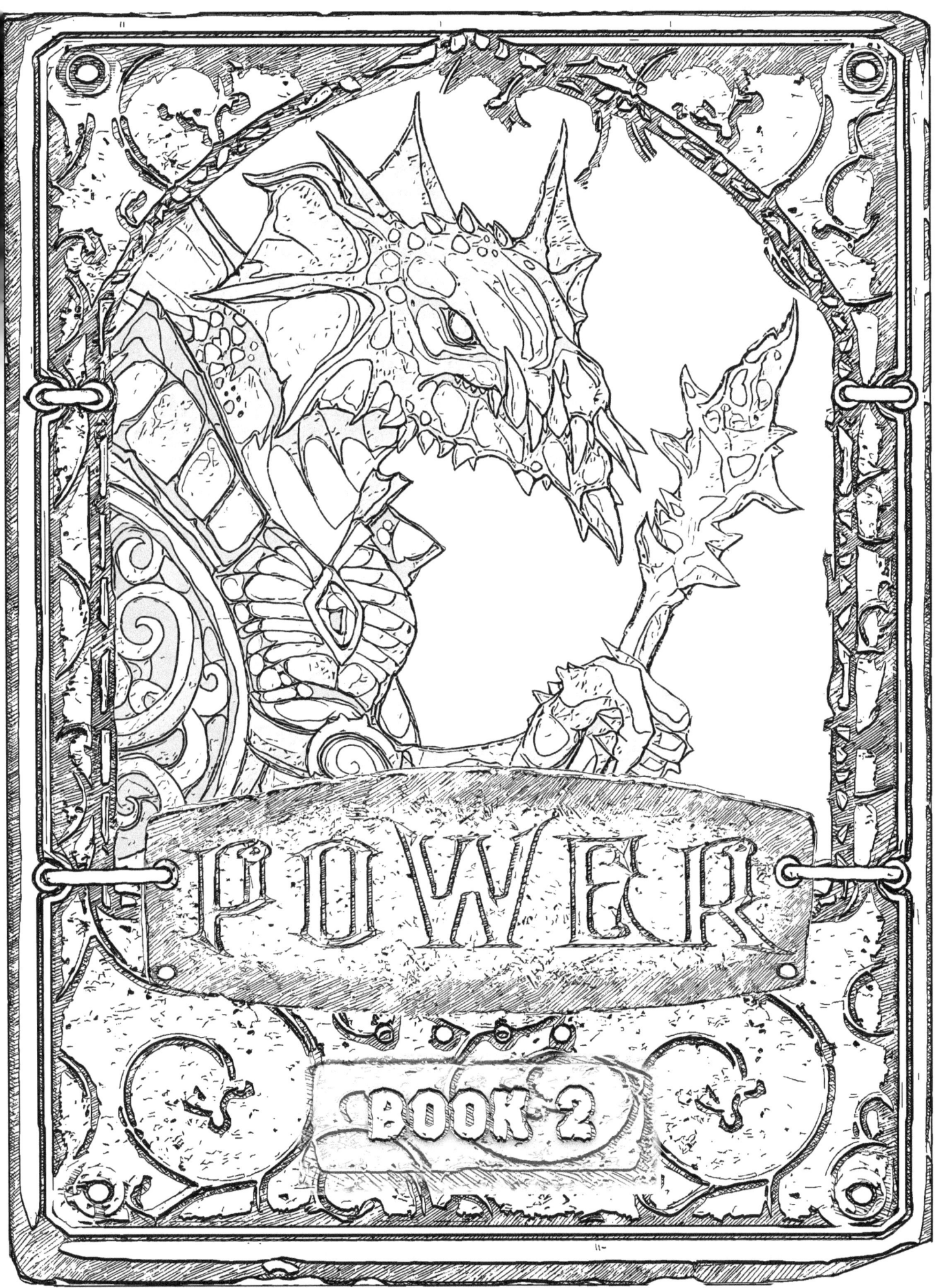

POWER

BOOK 2

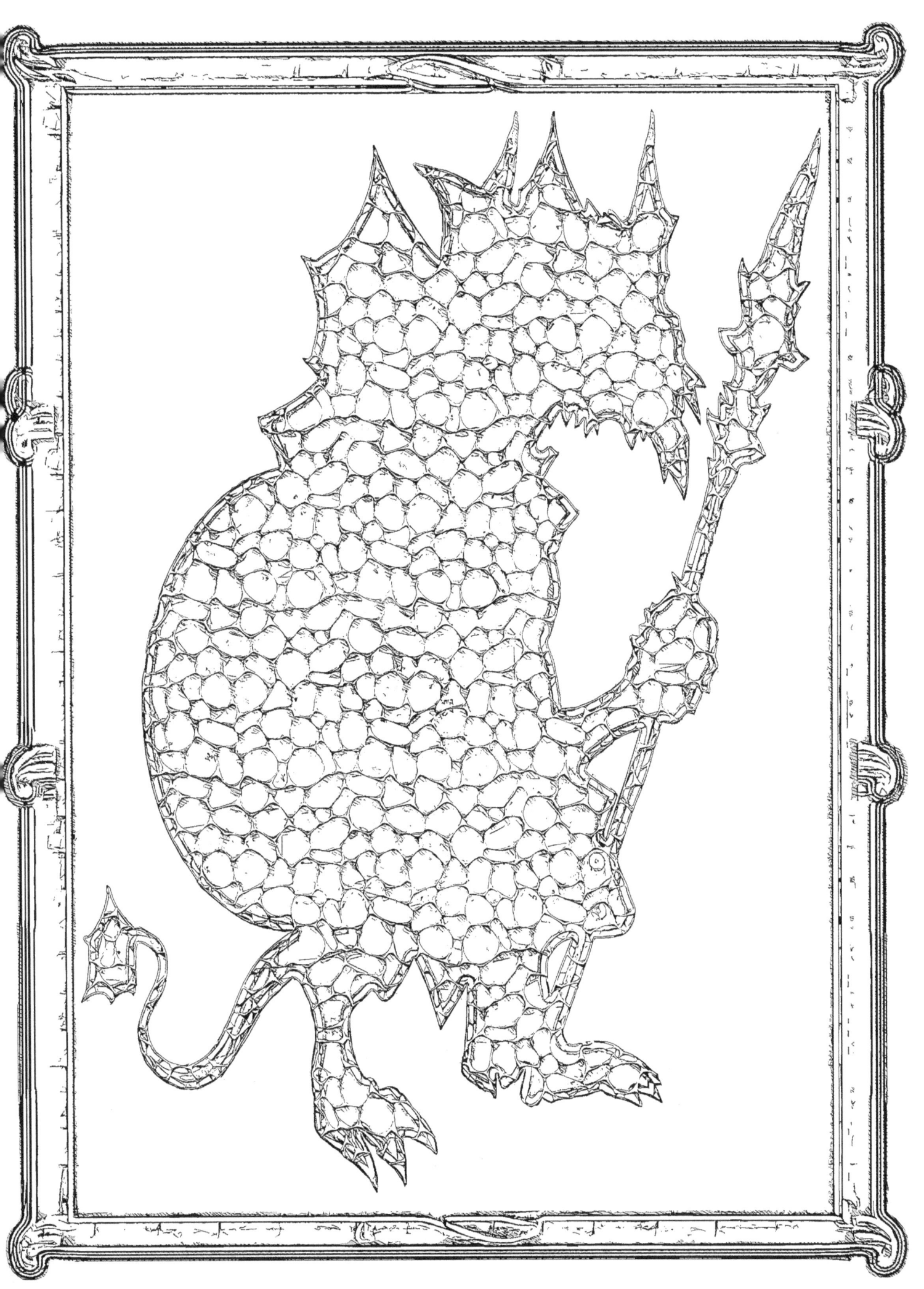

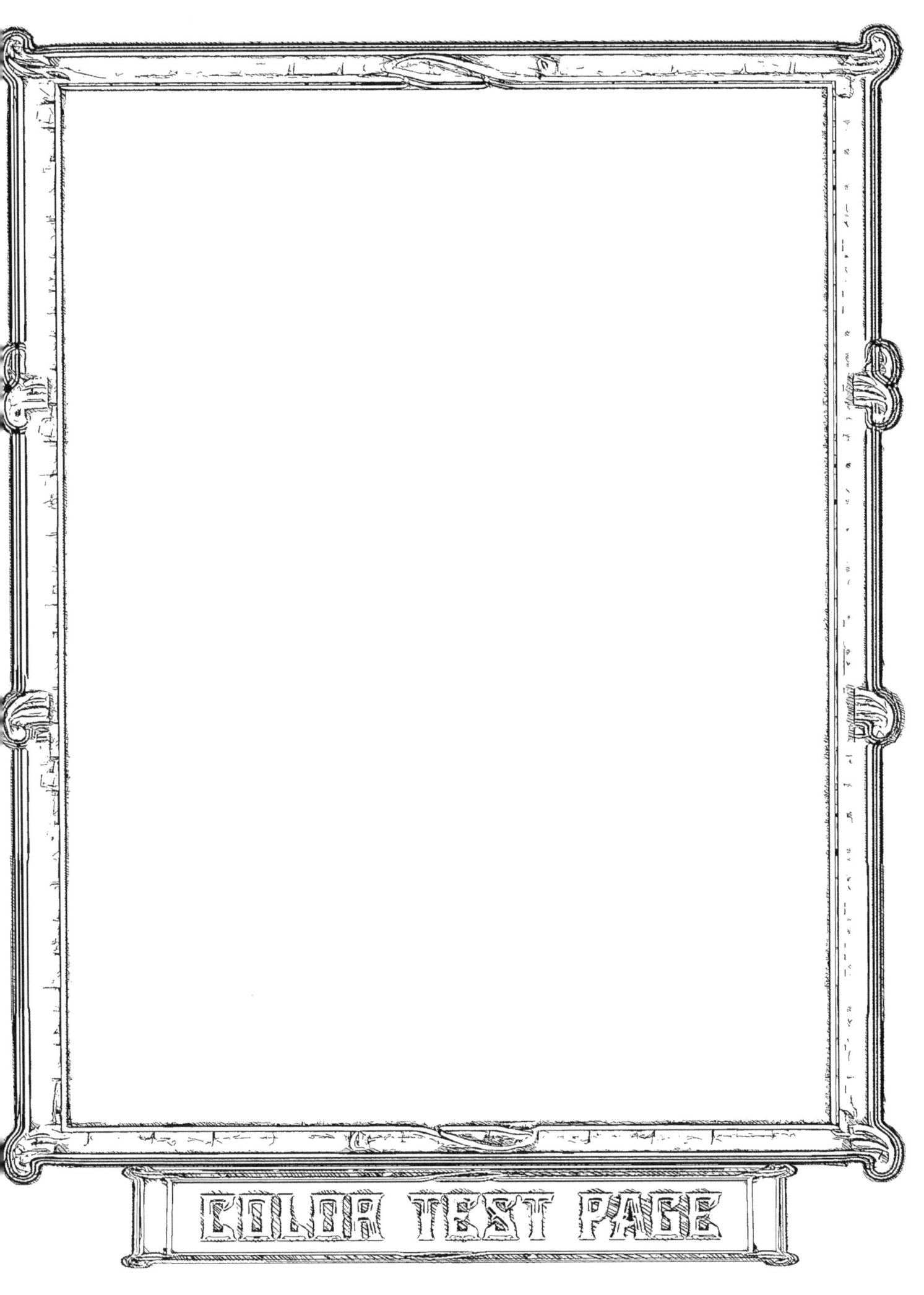

COLOR TEST PAGE

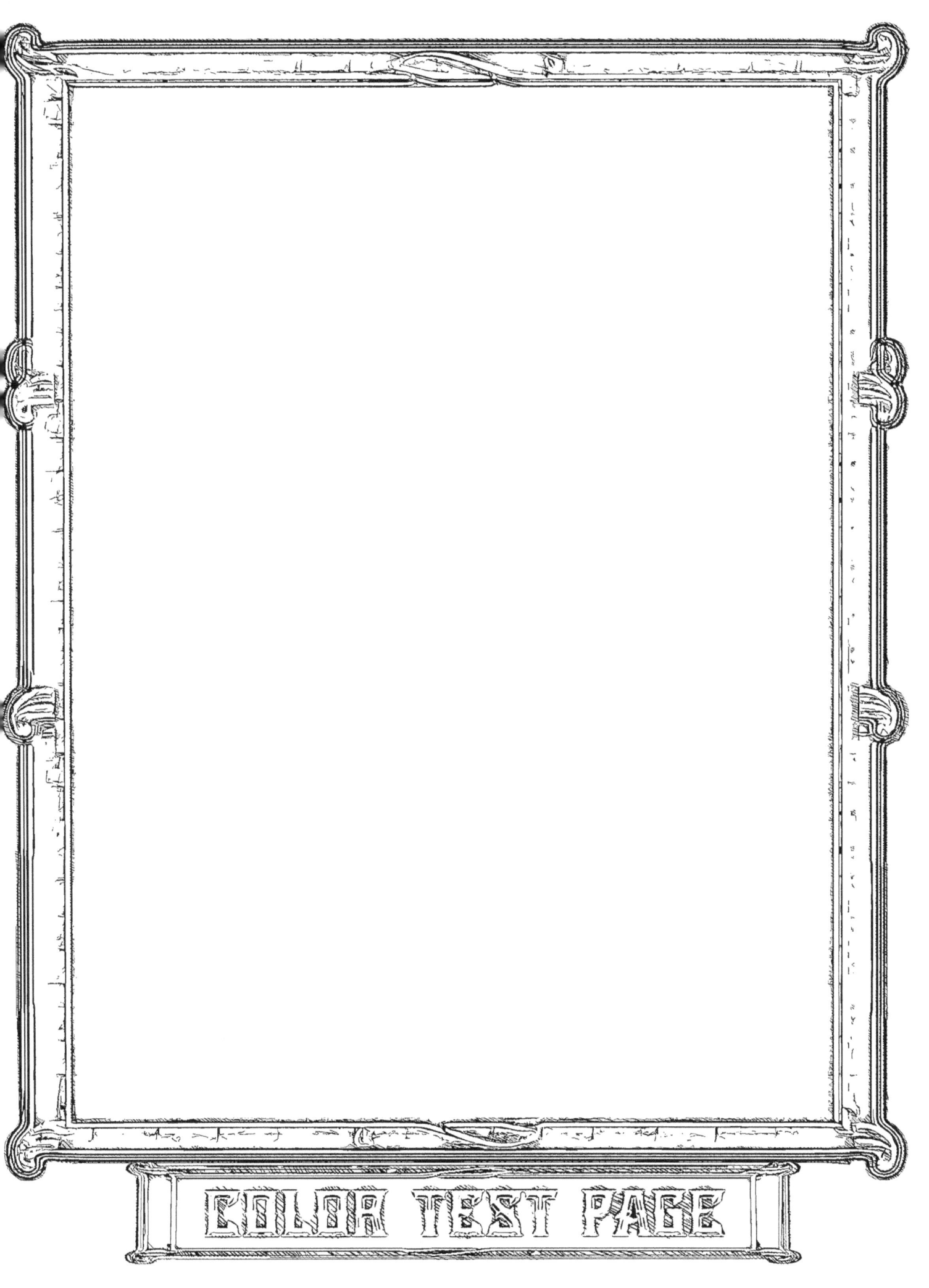

COLOR TEST PAGE

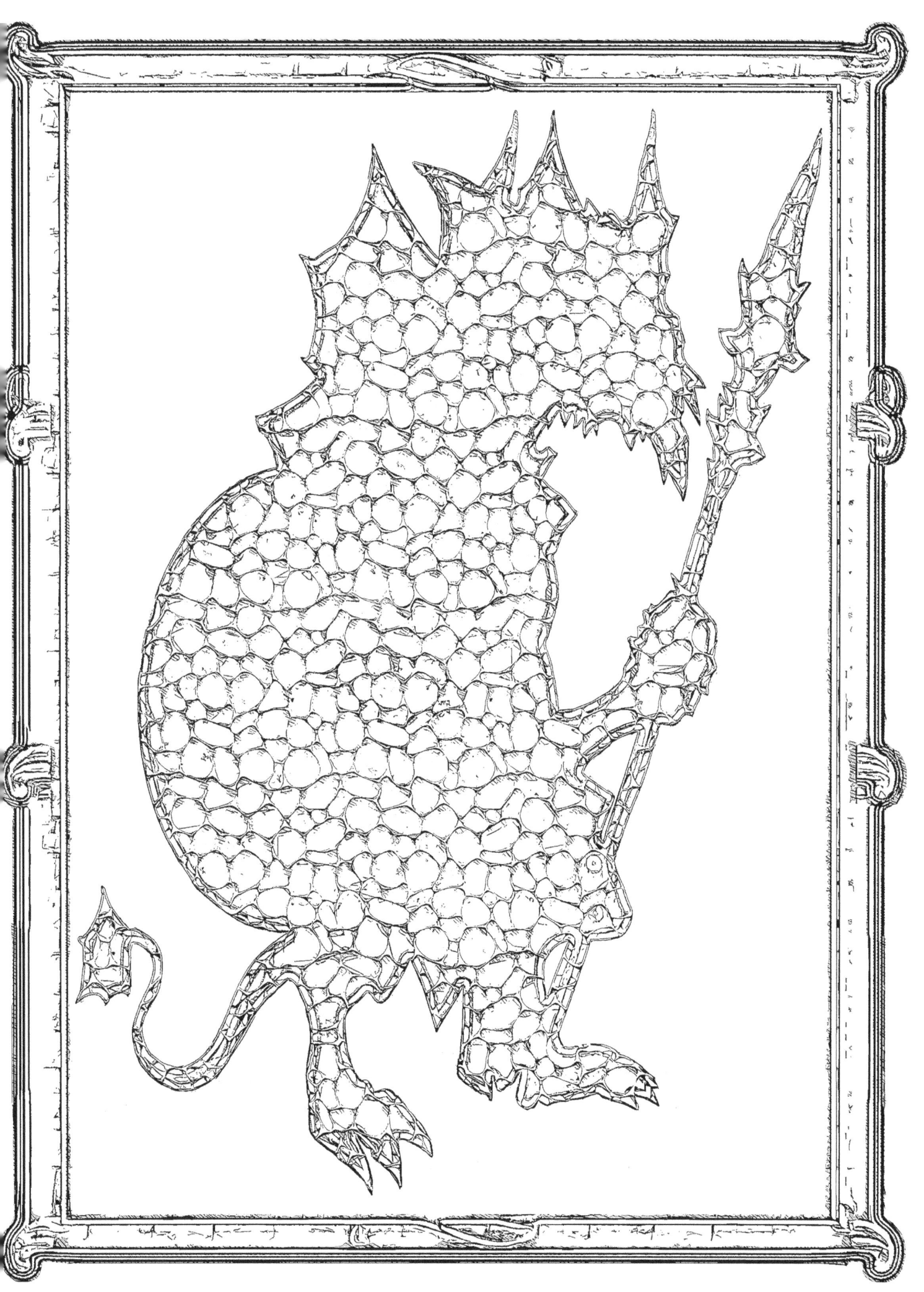

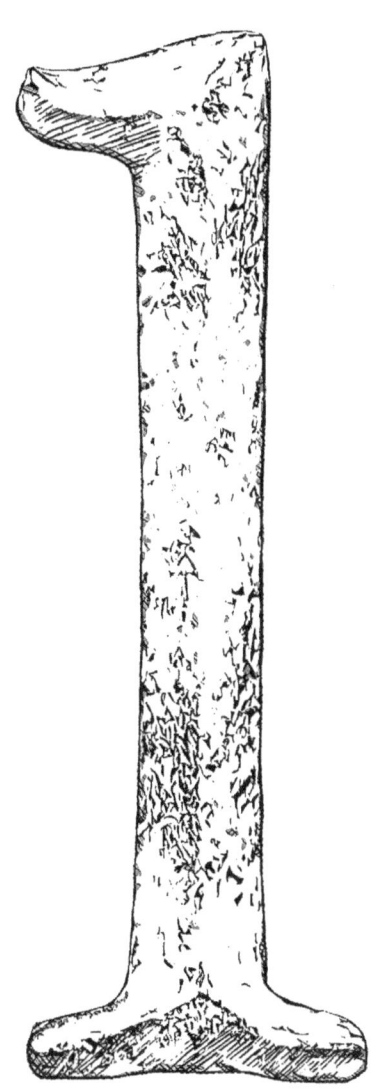

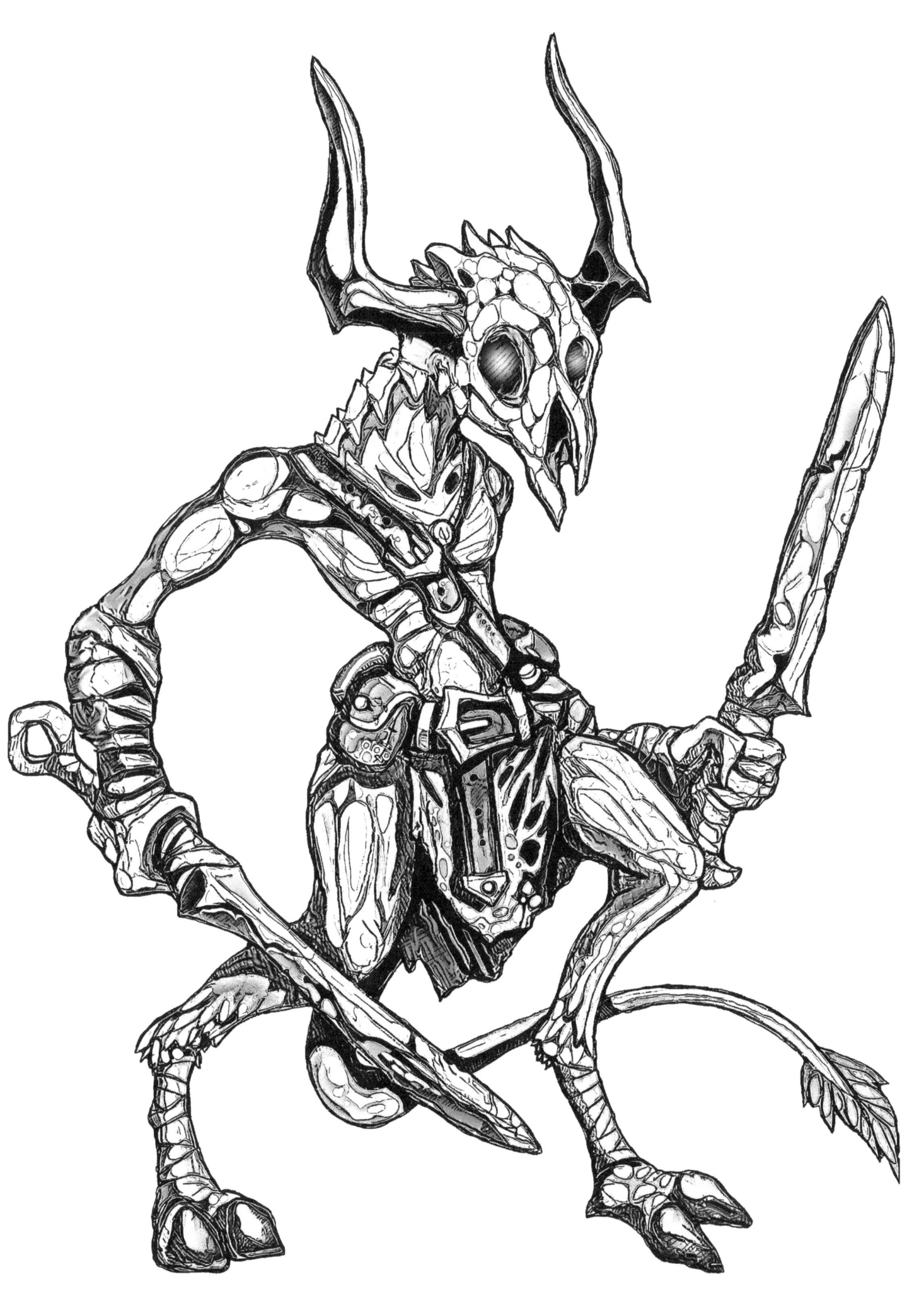

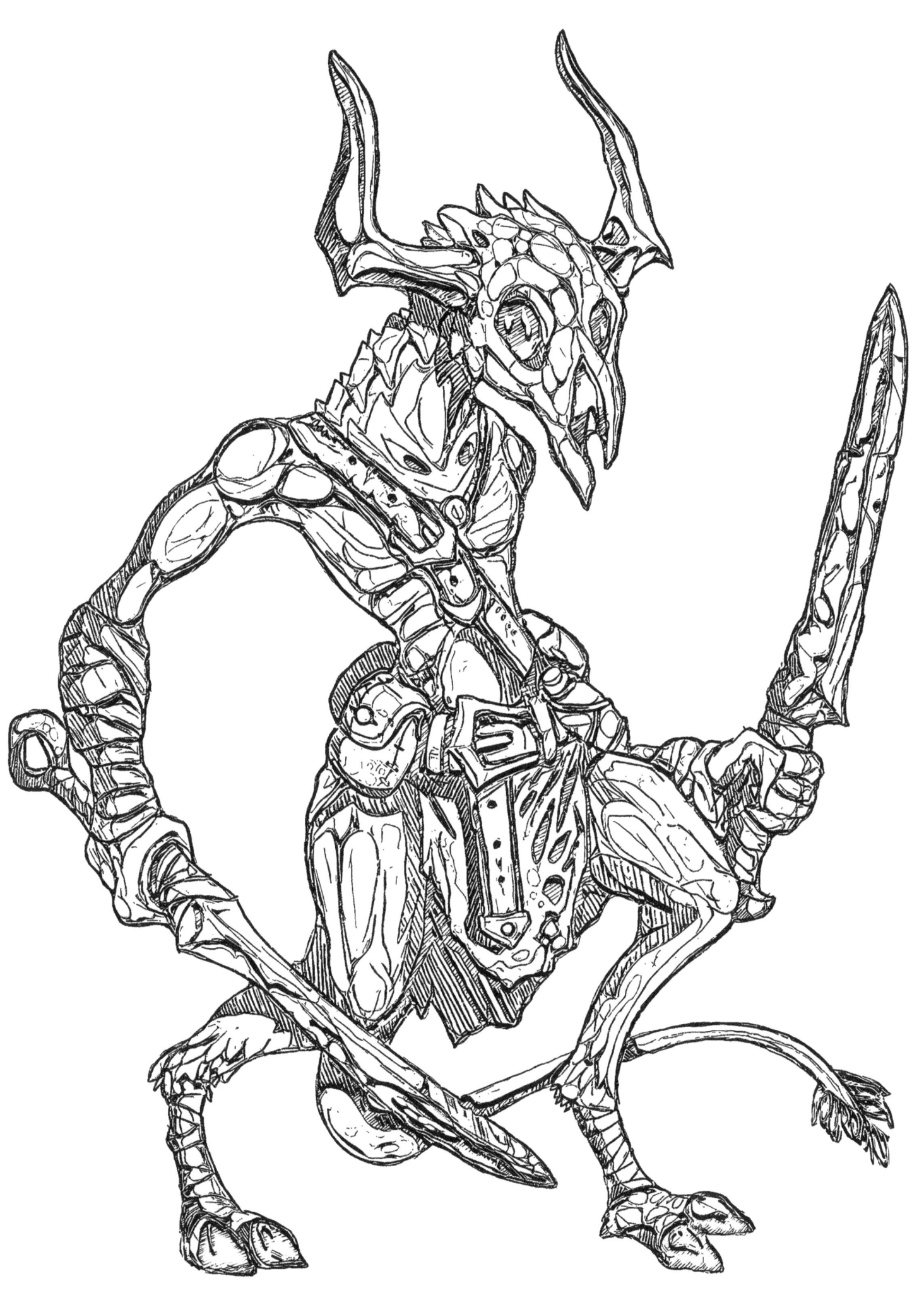

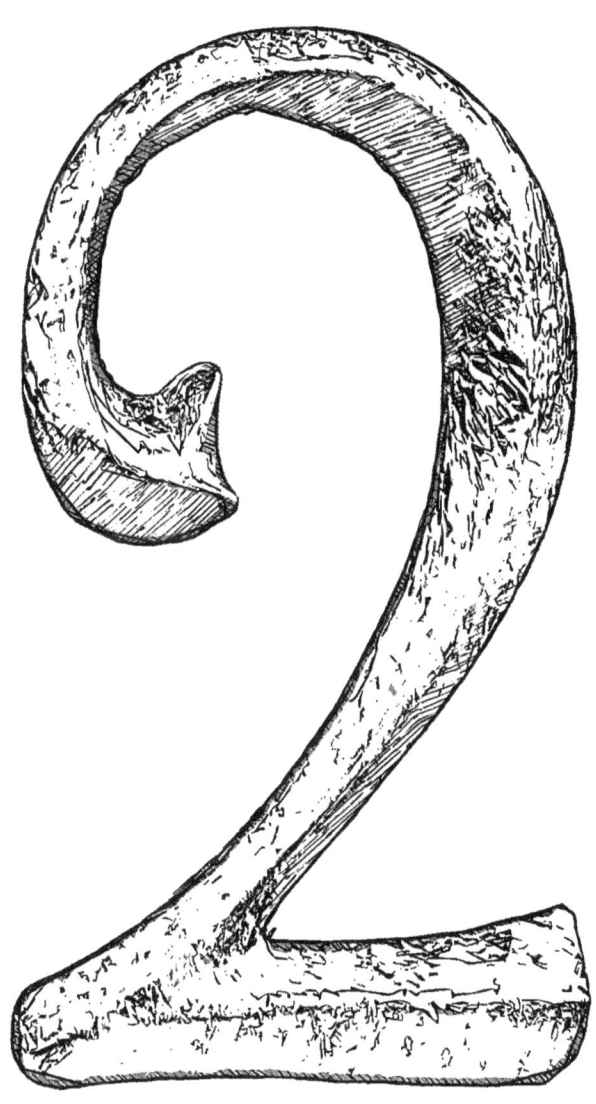

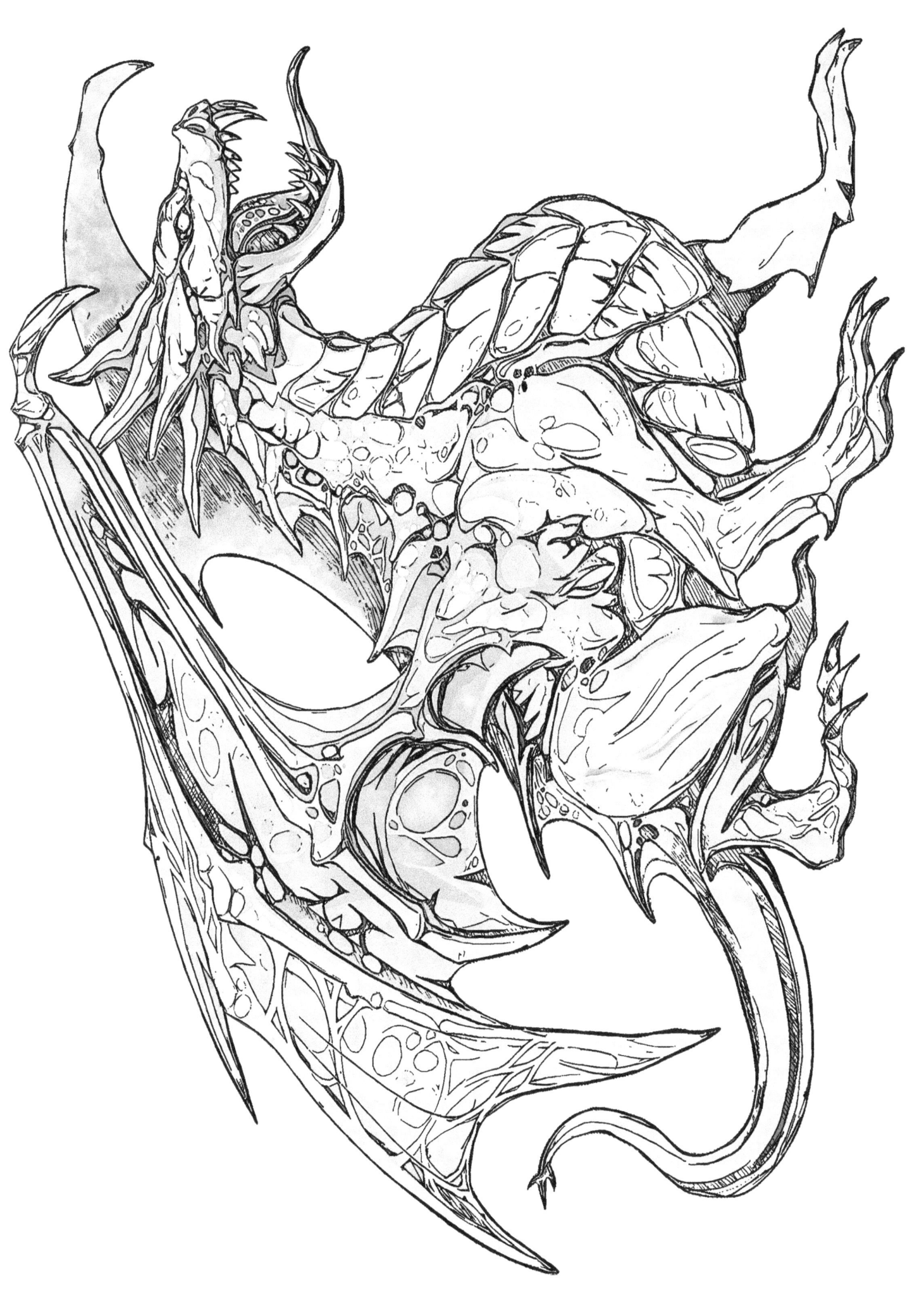

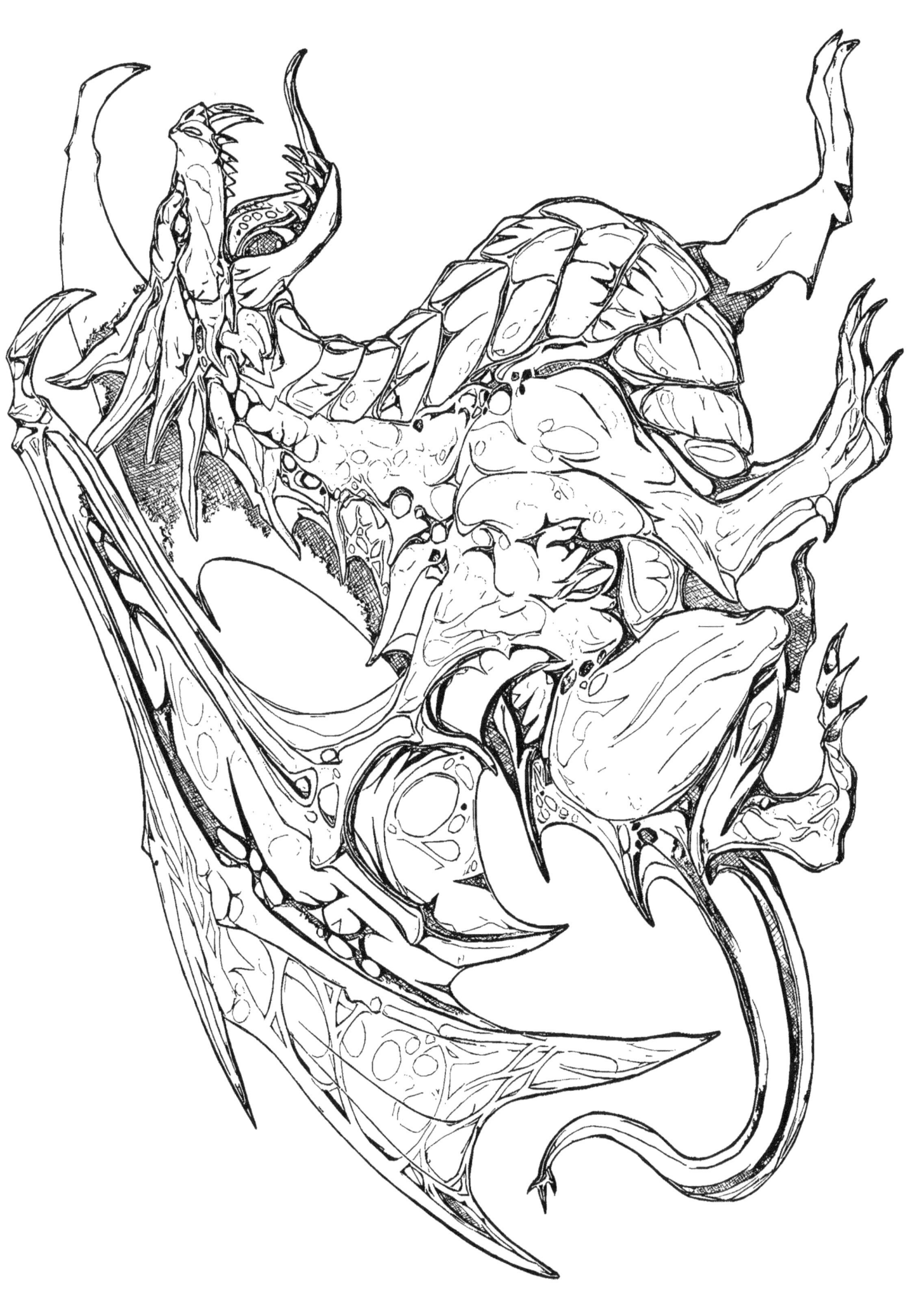

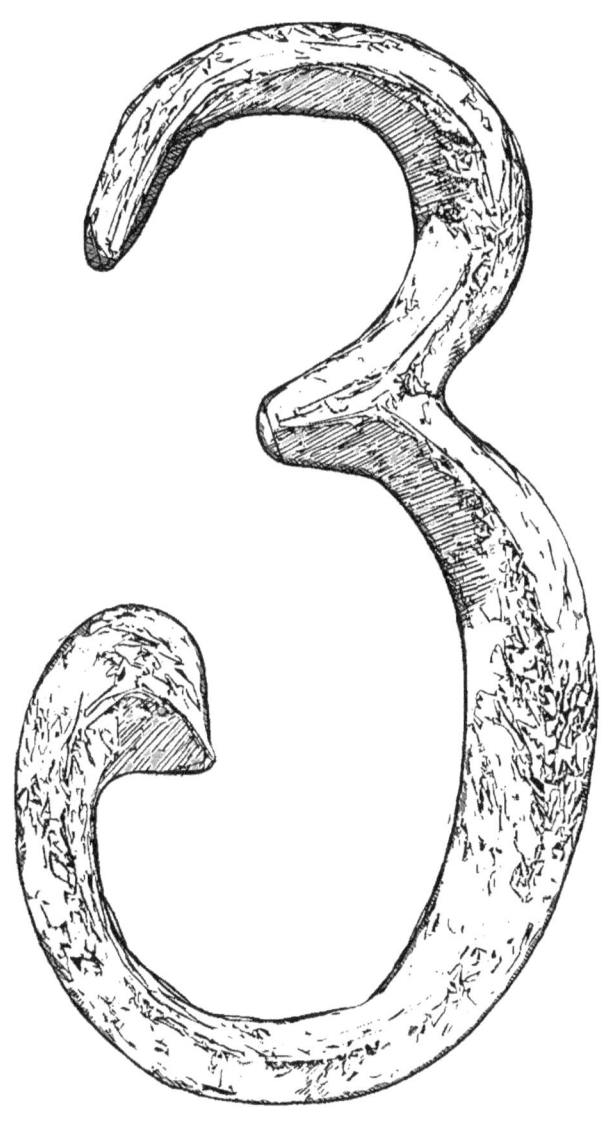

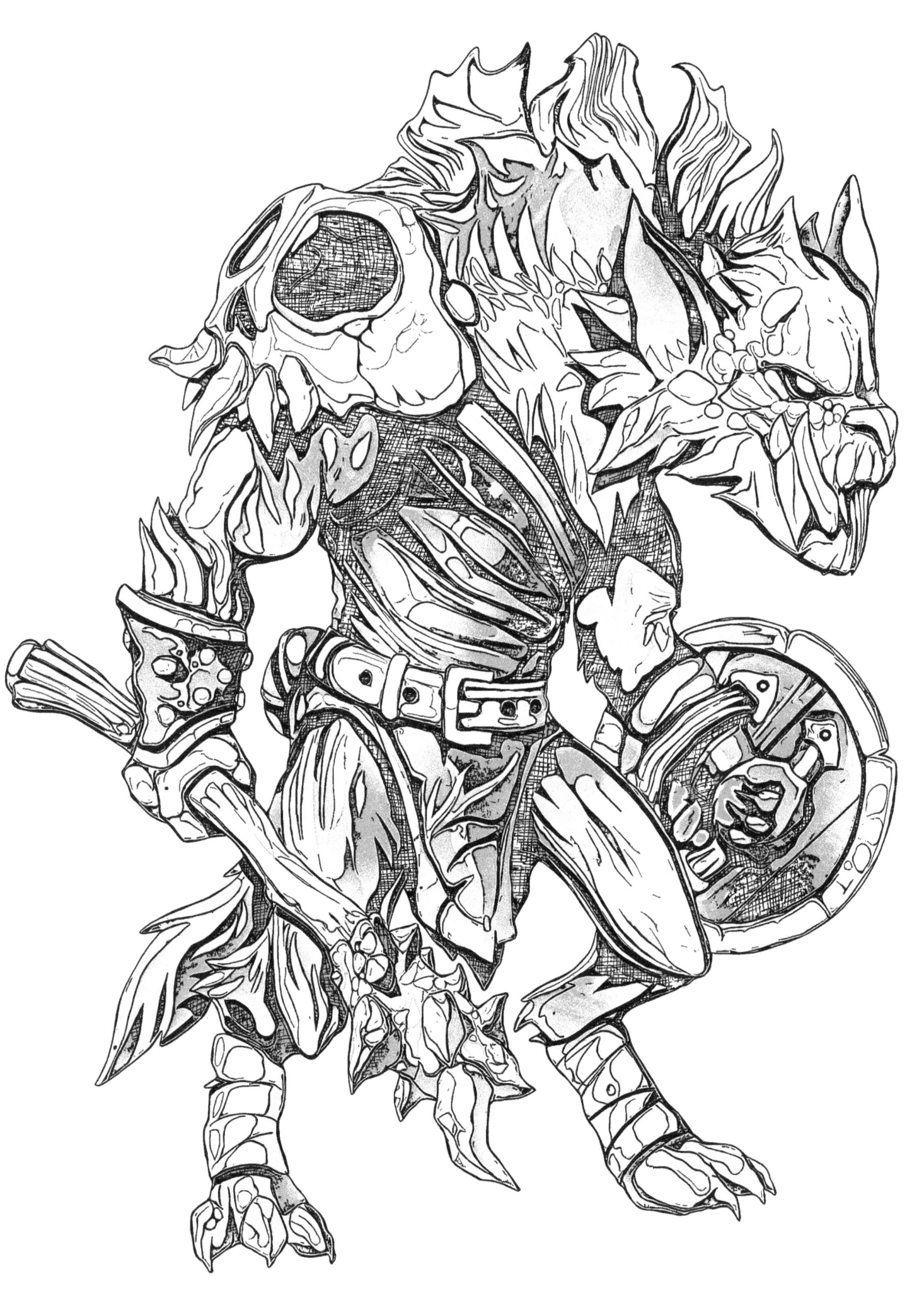

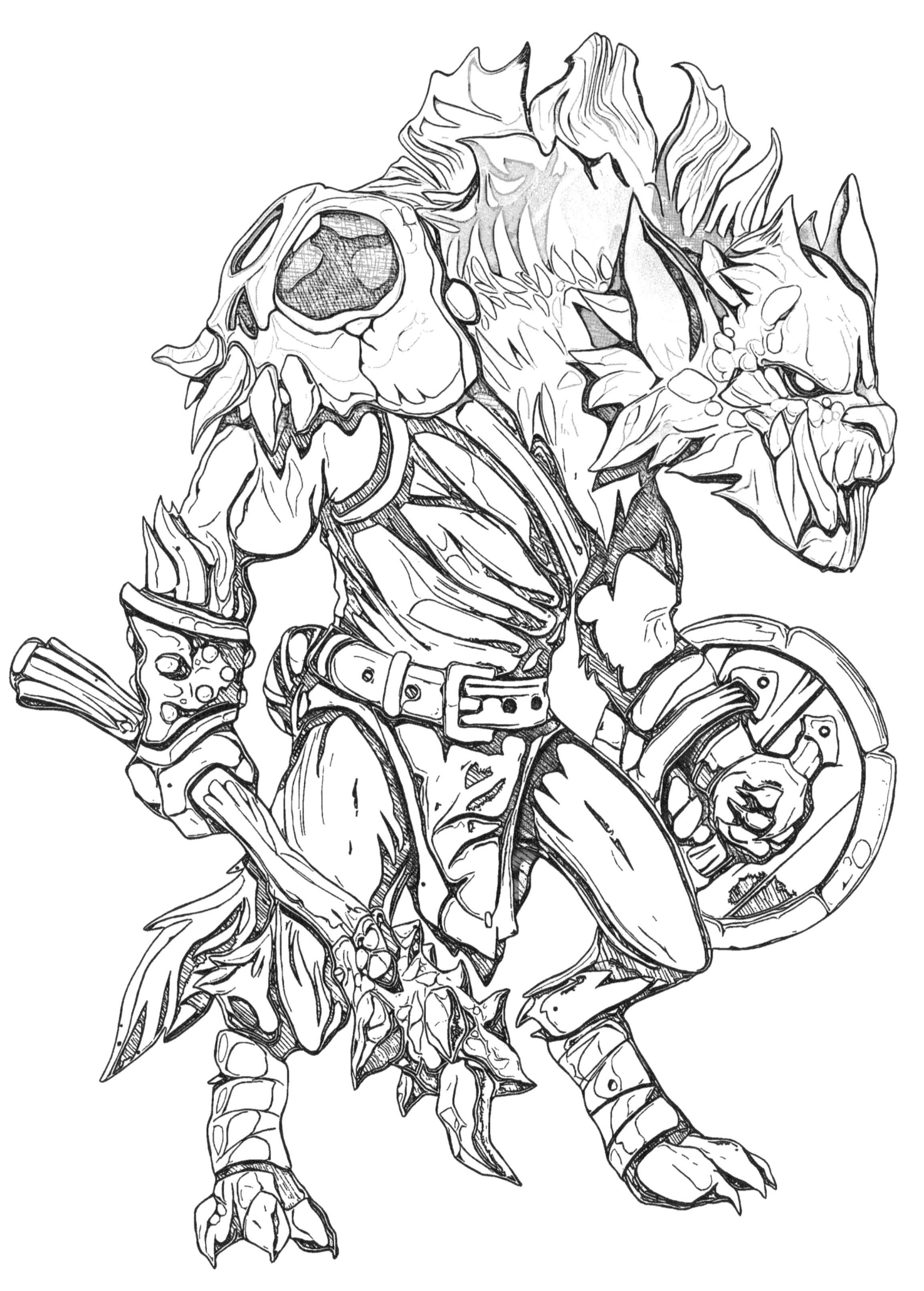

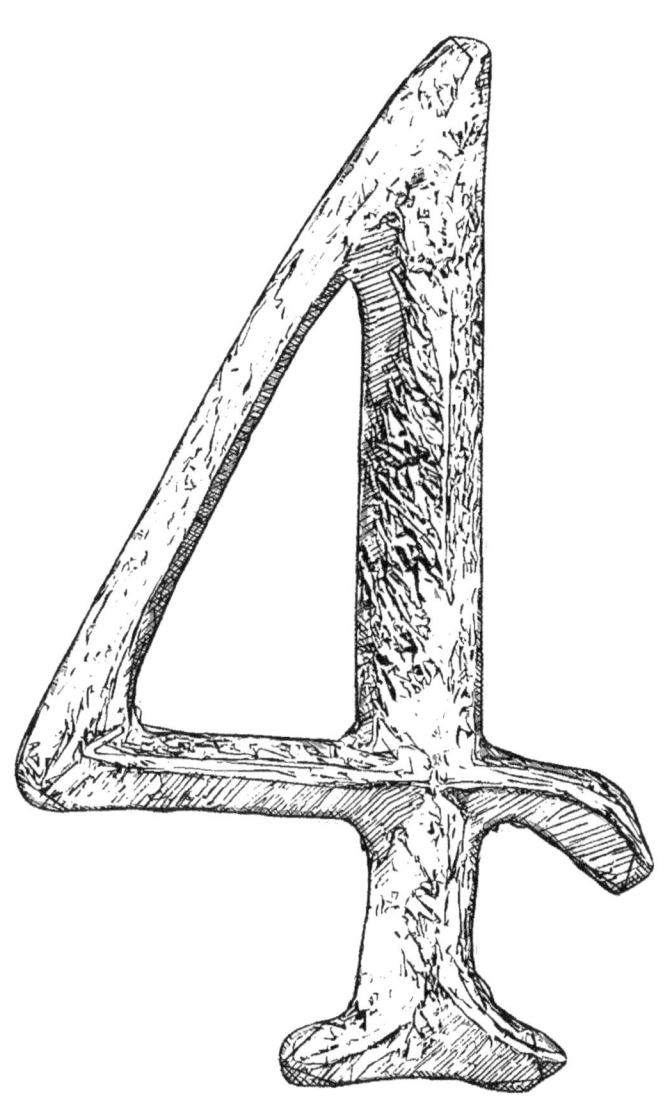

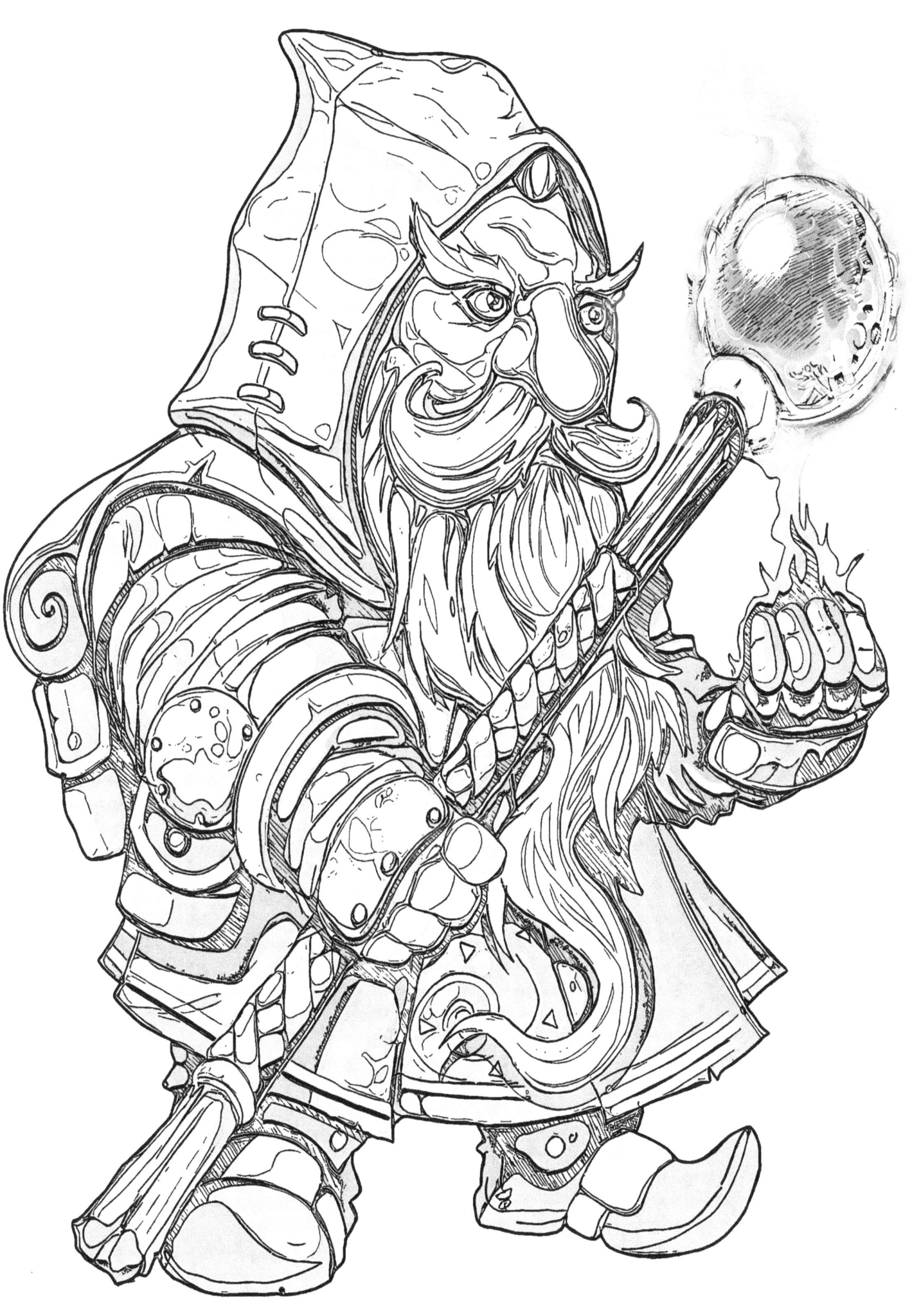

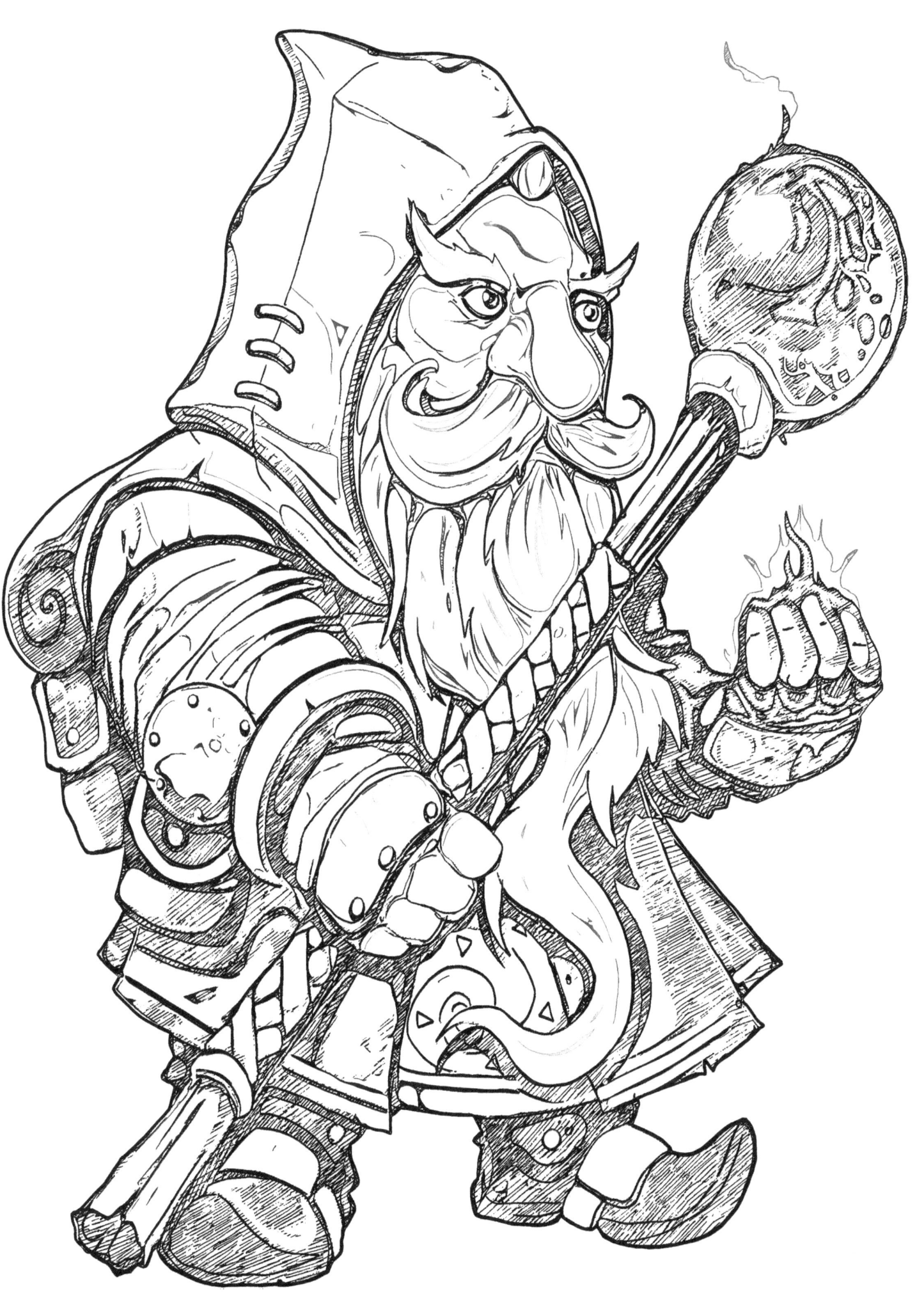

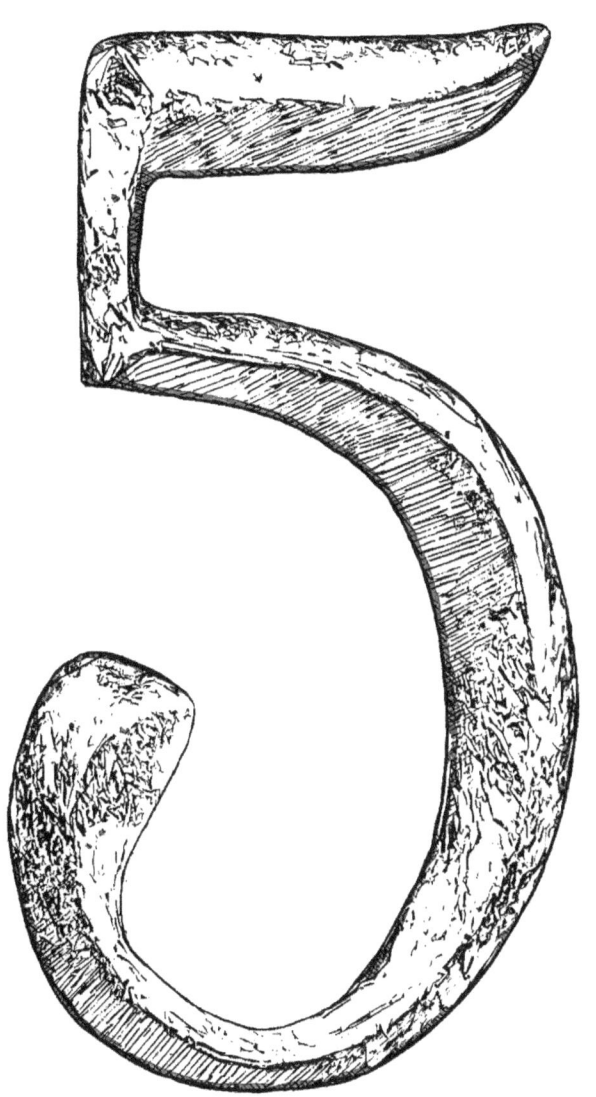

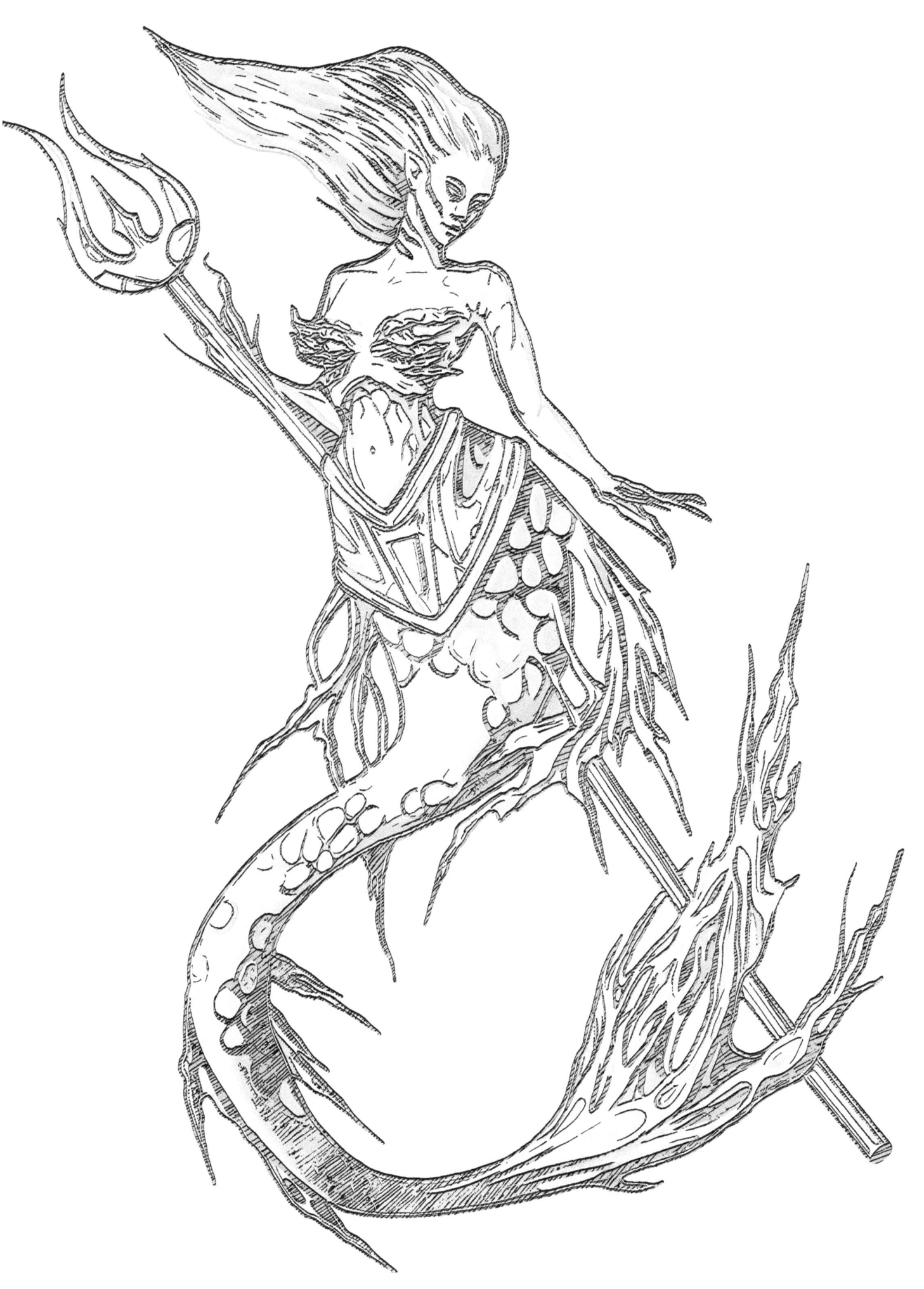

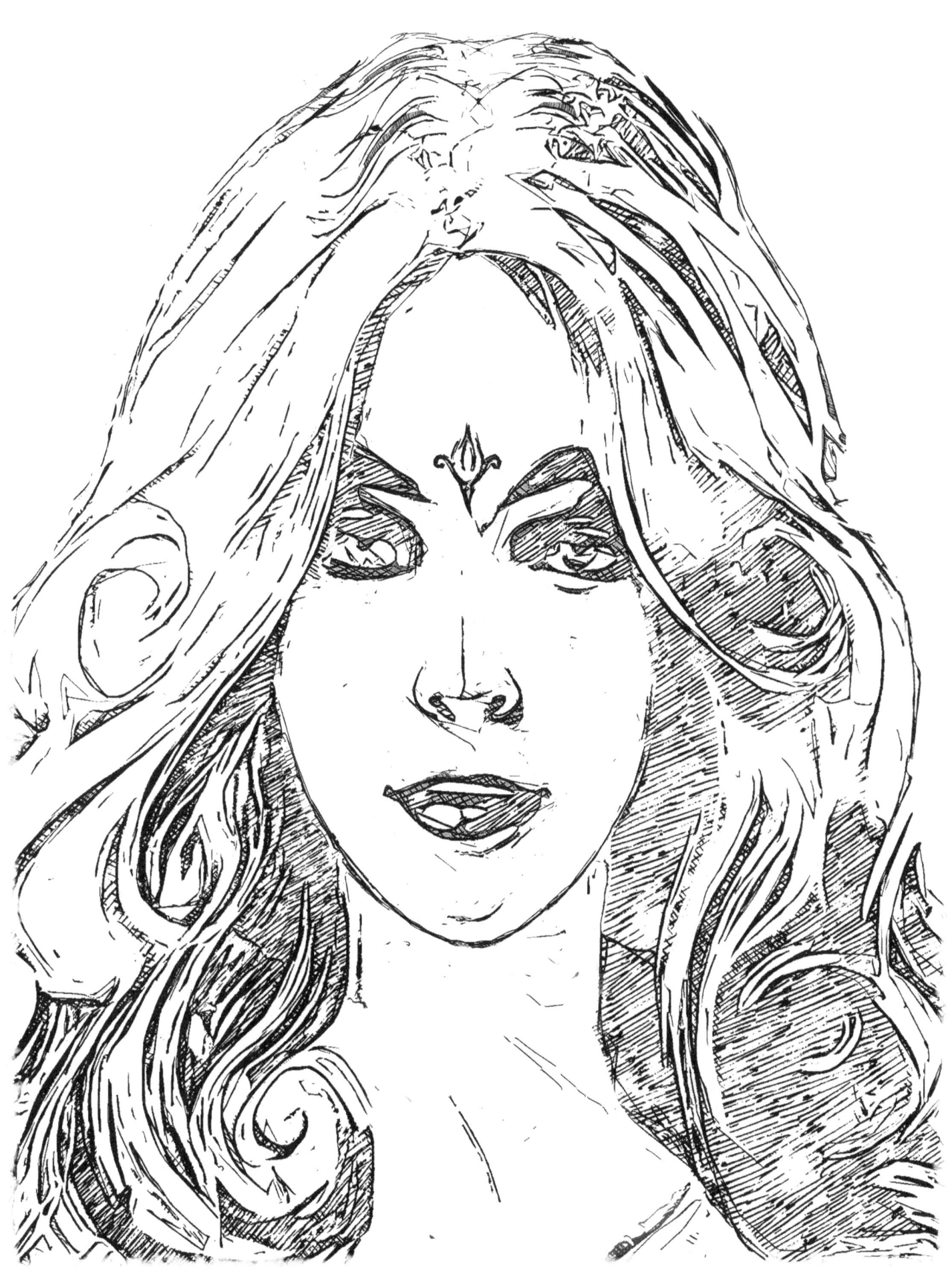

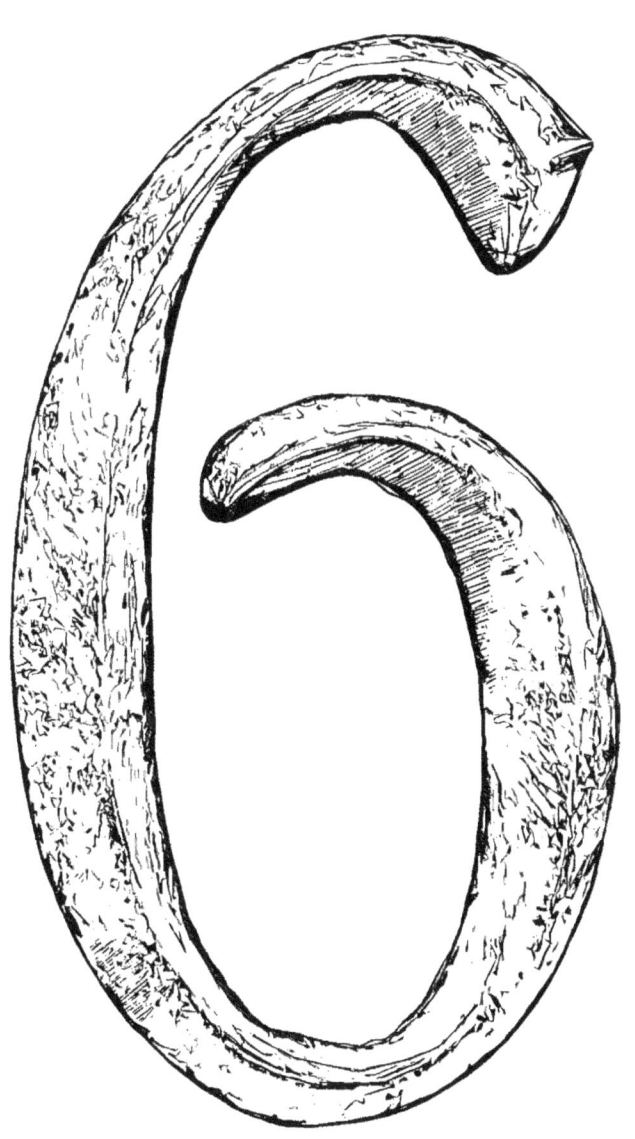

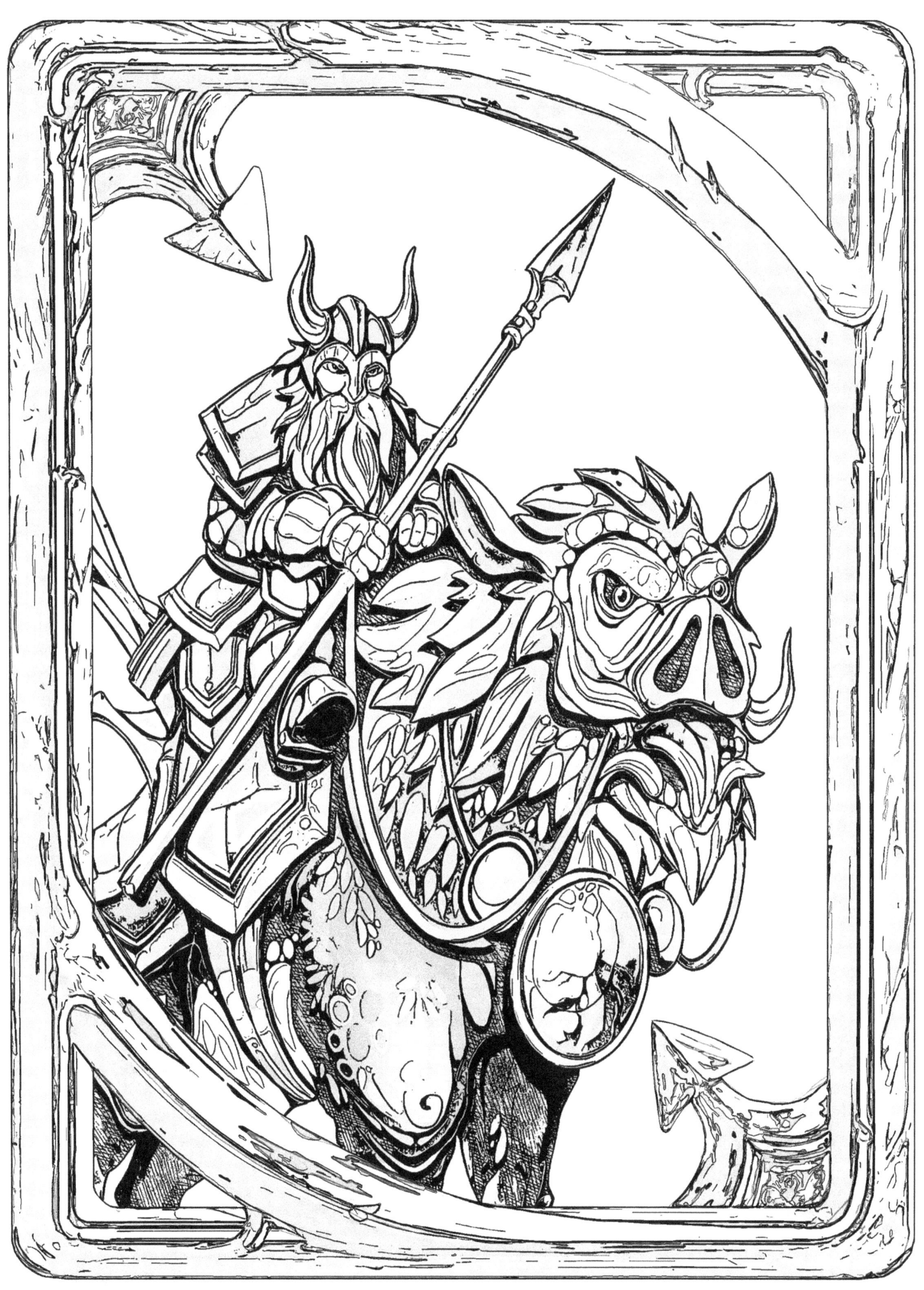

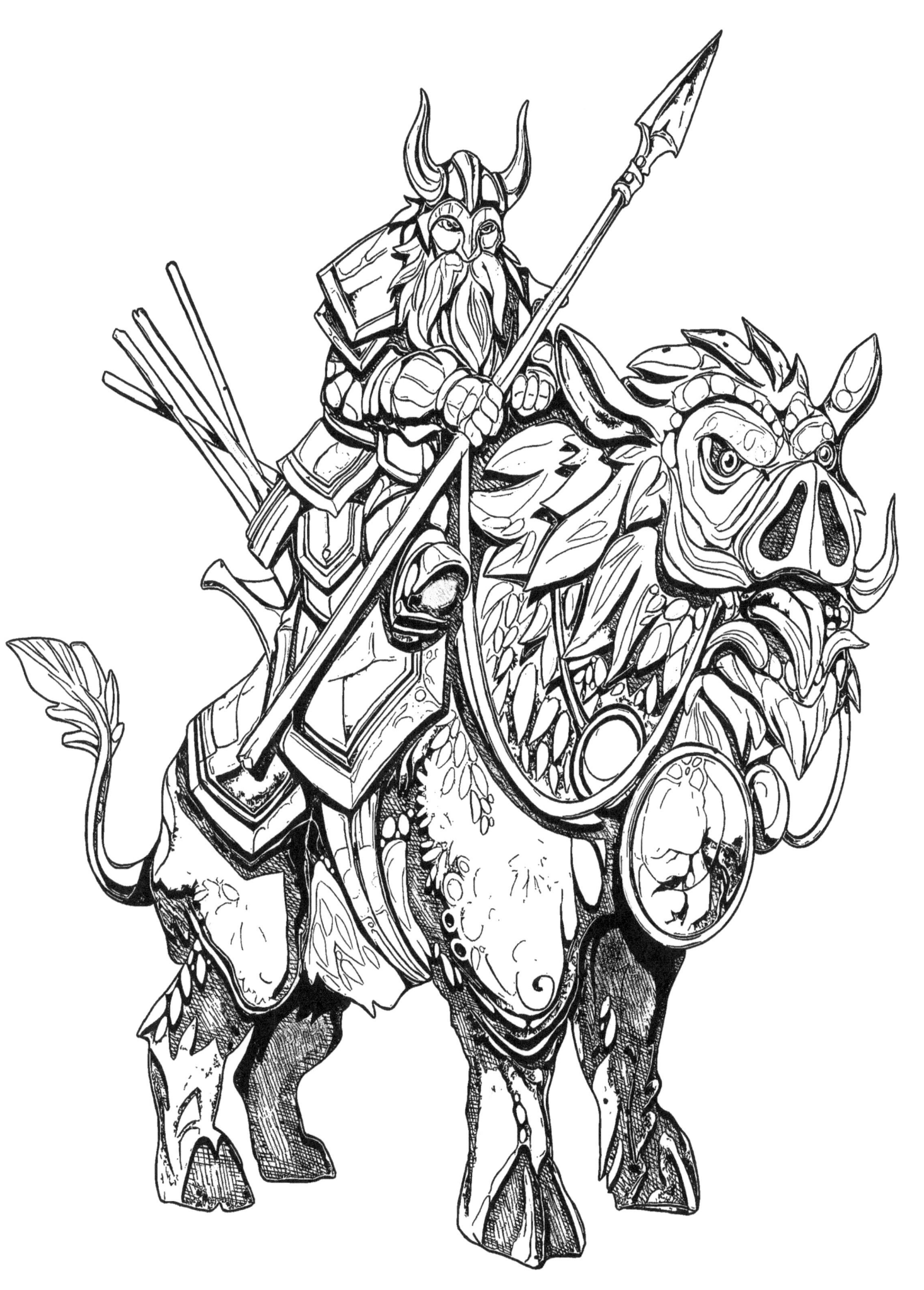

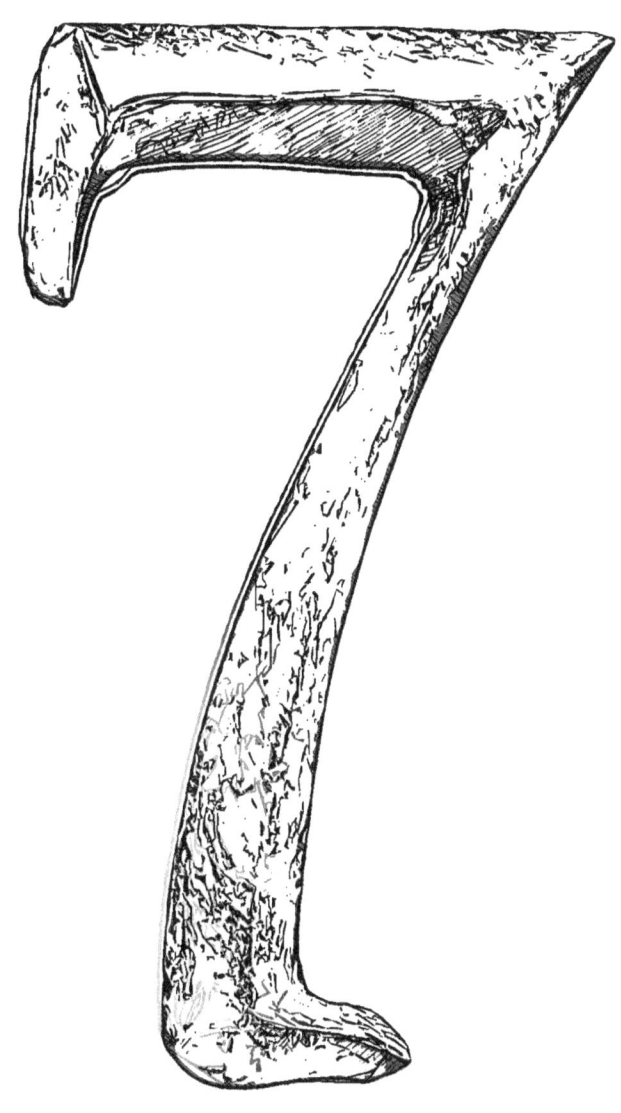

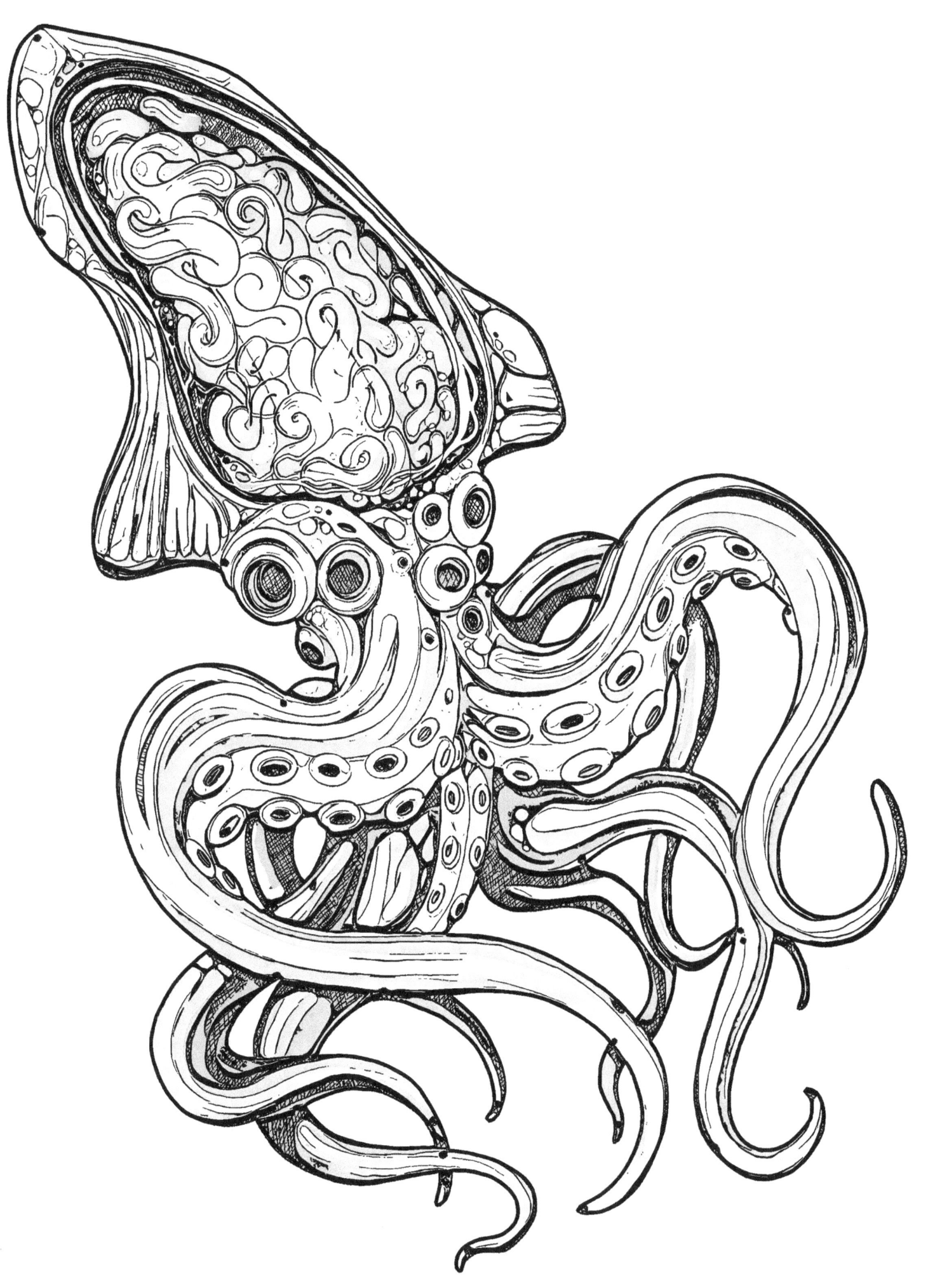

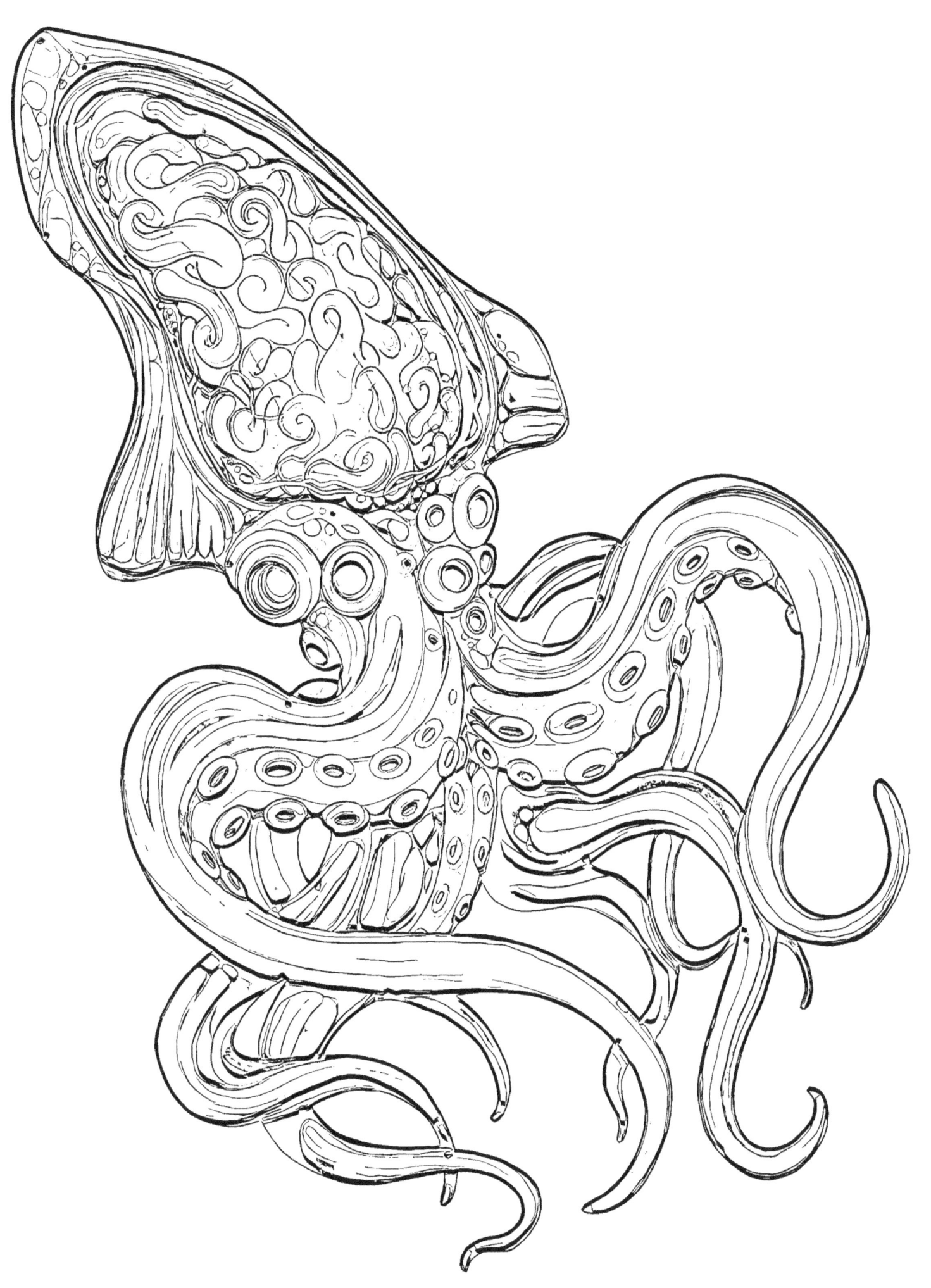

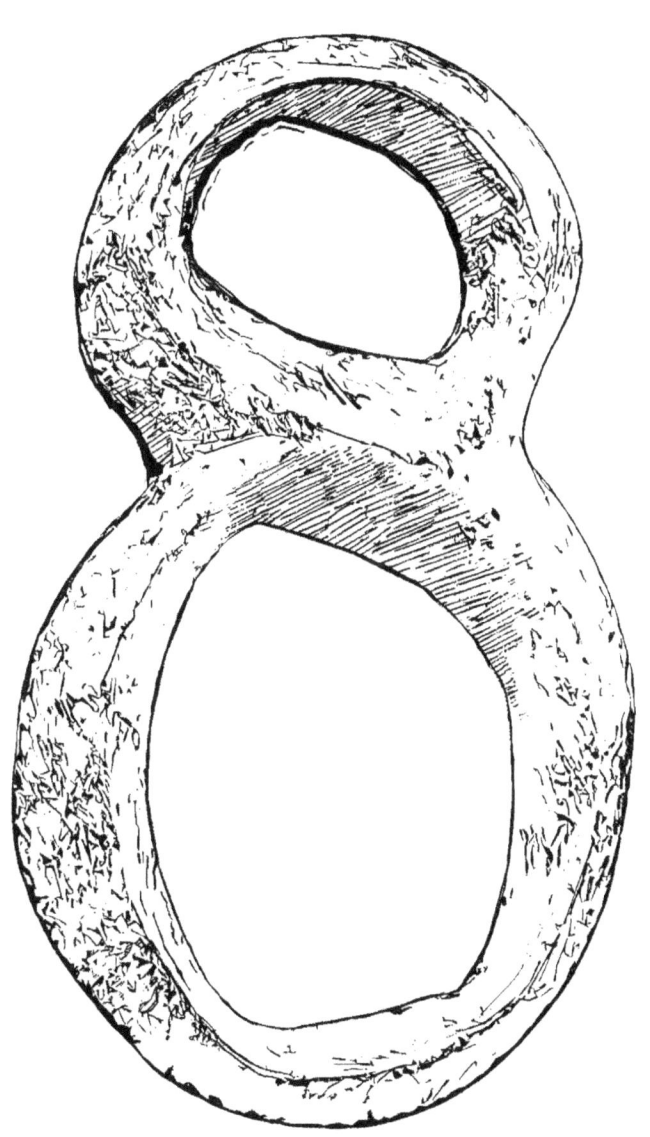

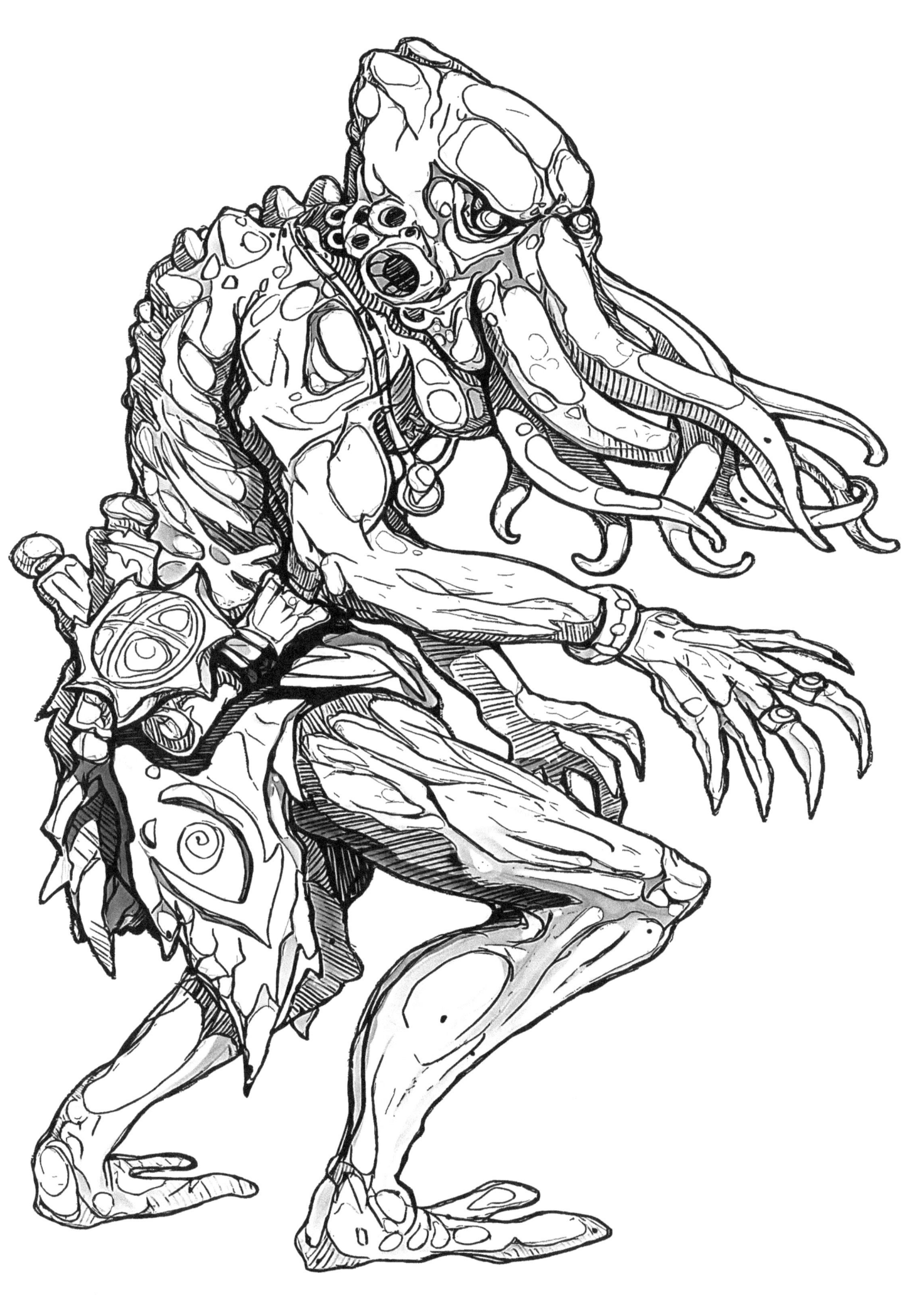

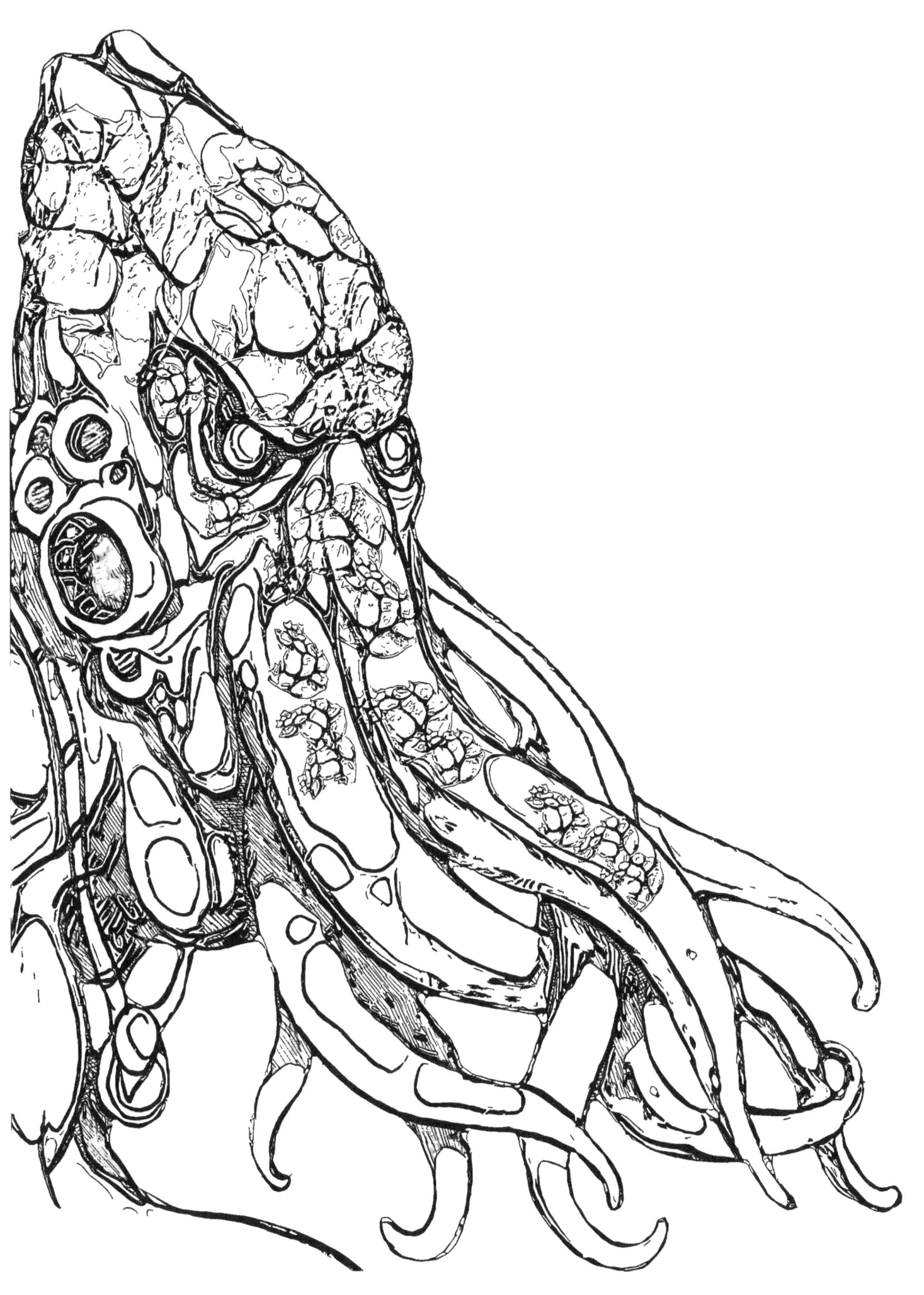

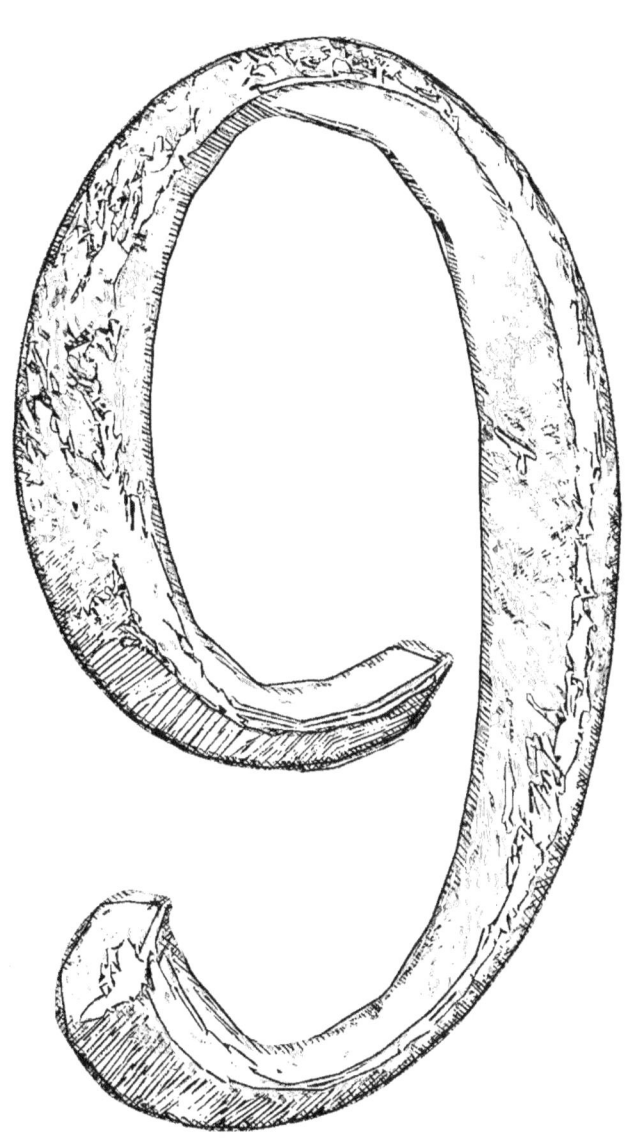

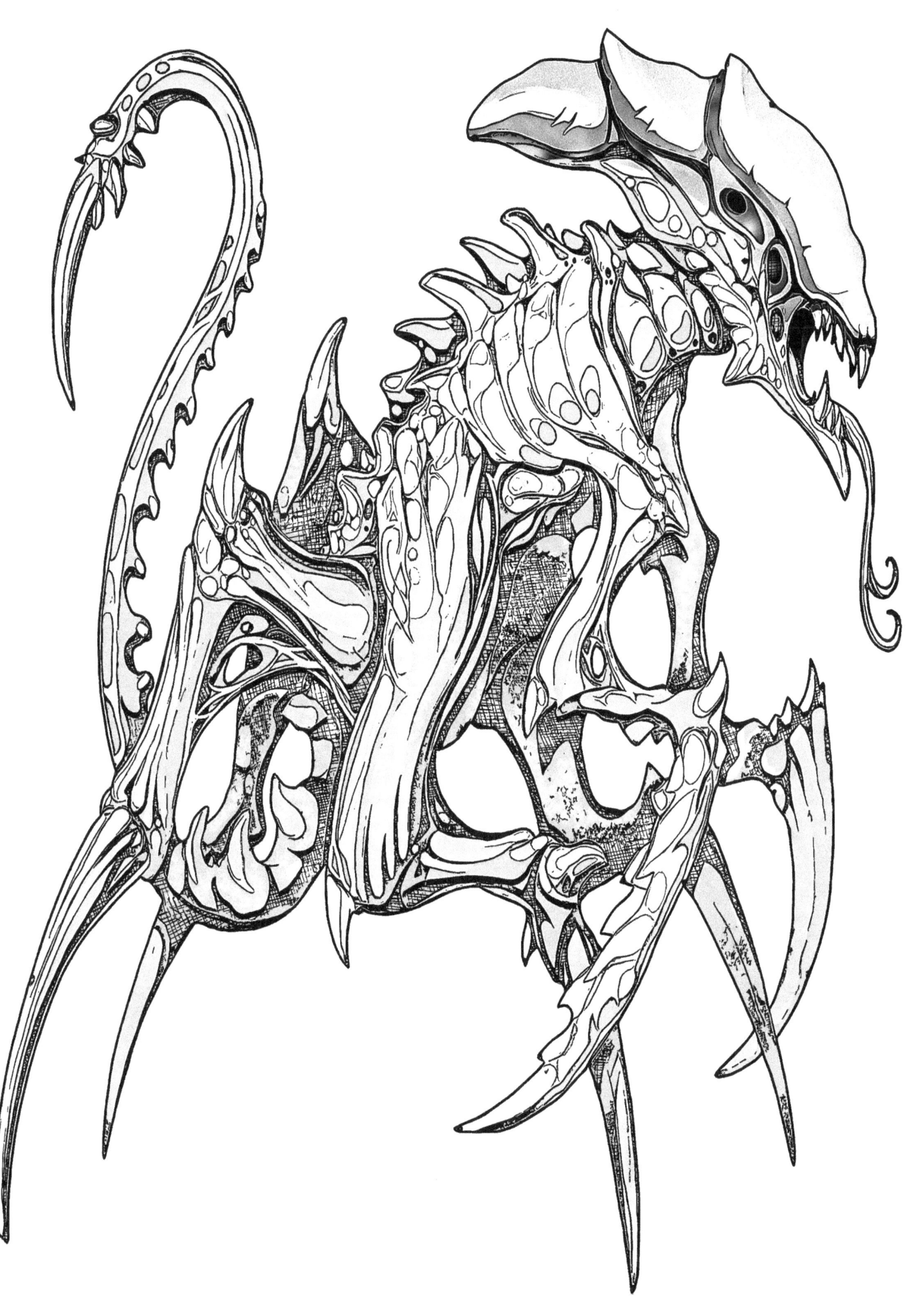

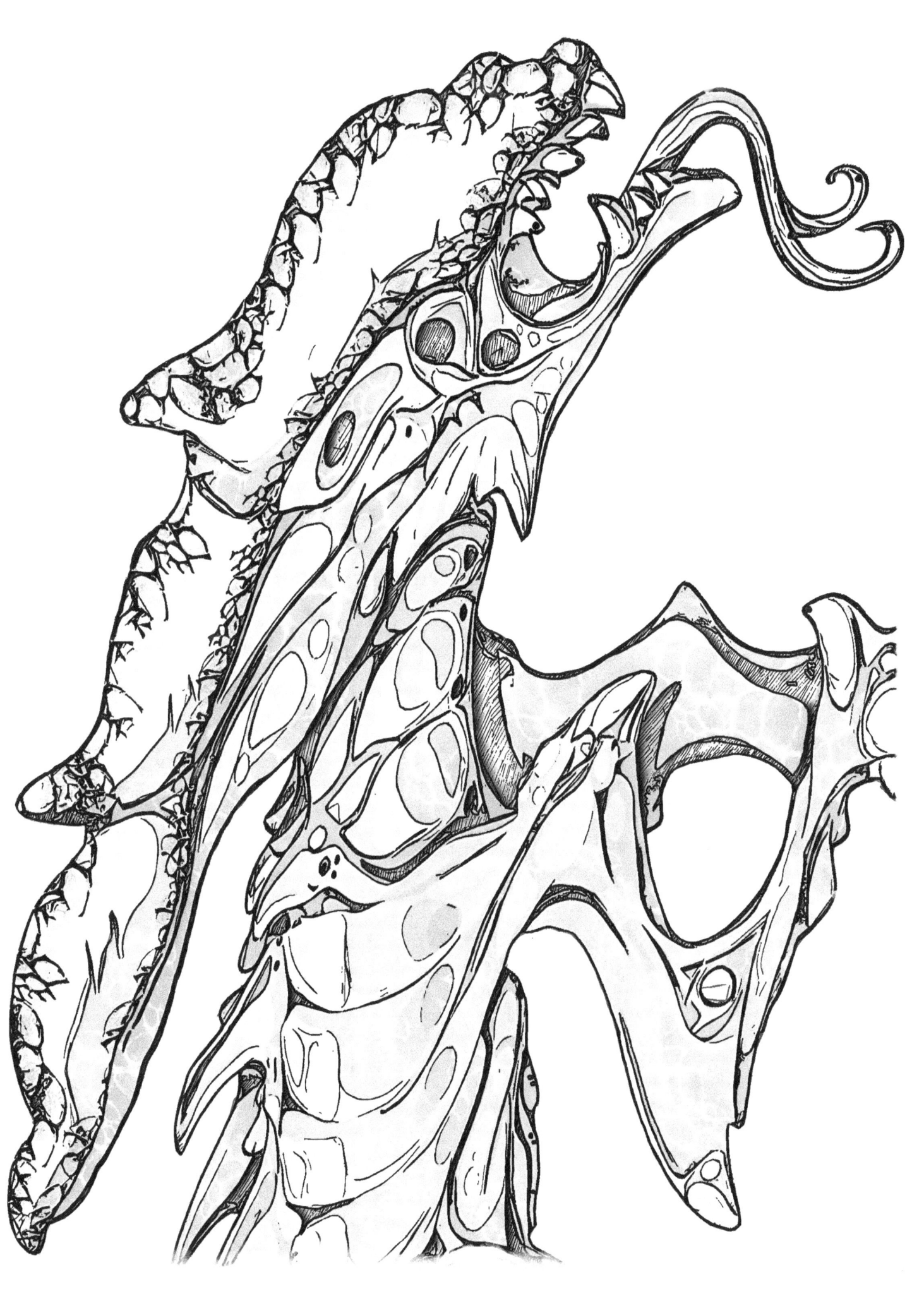

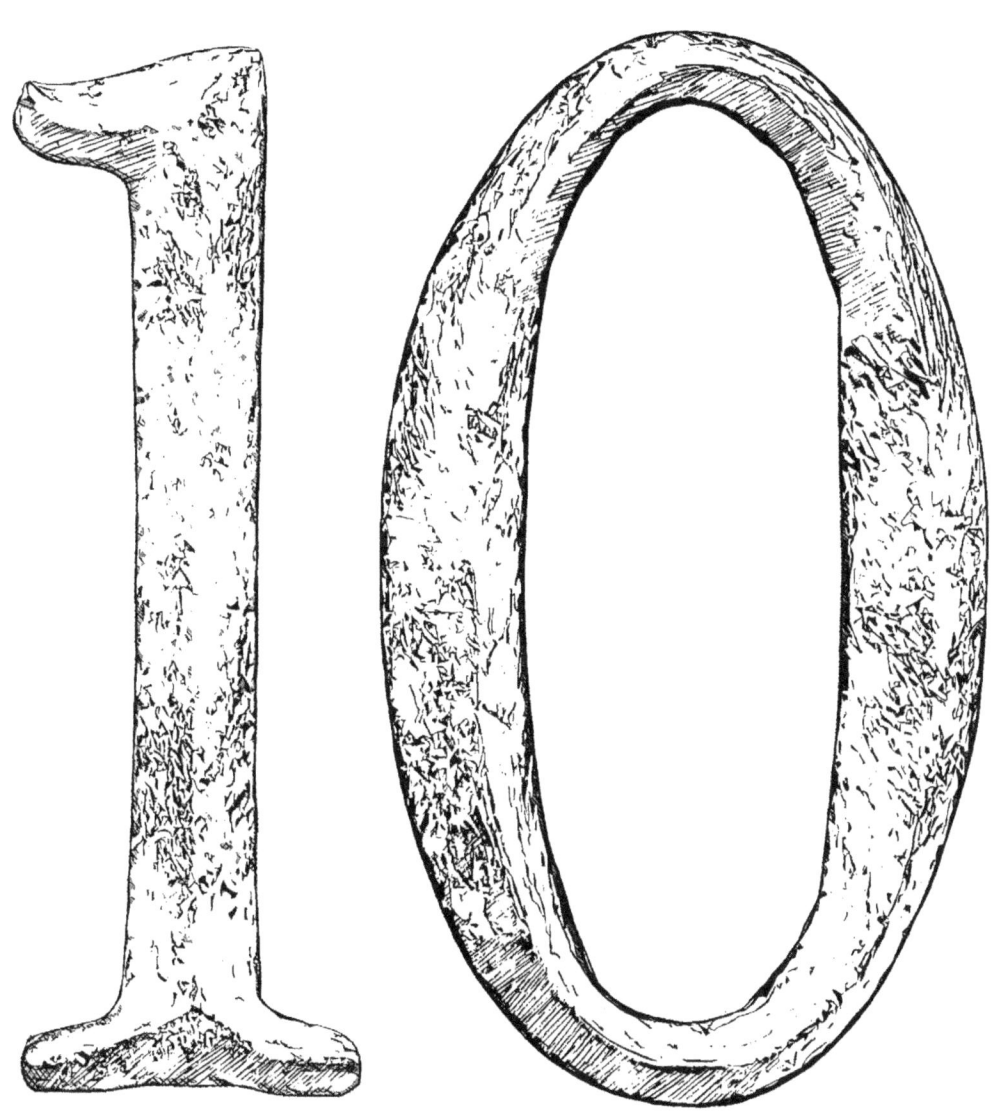

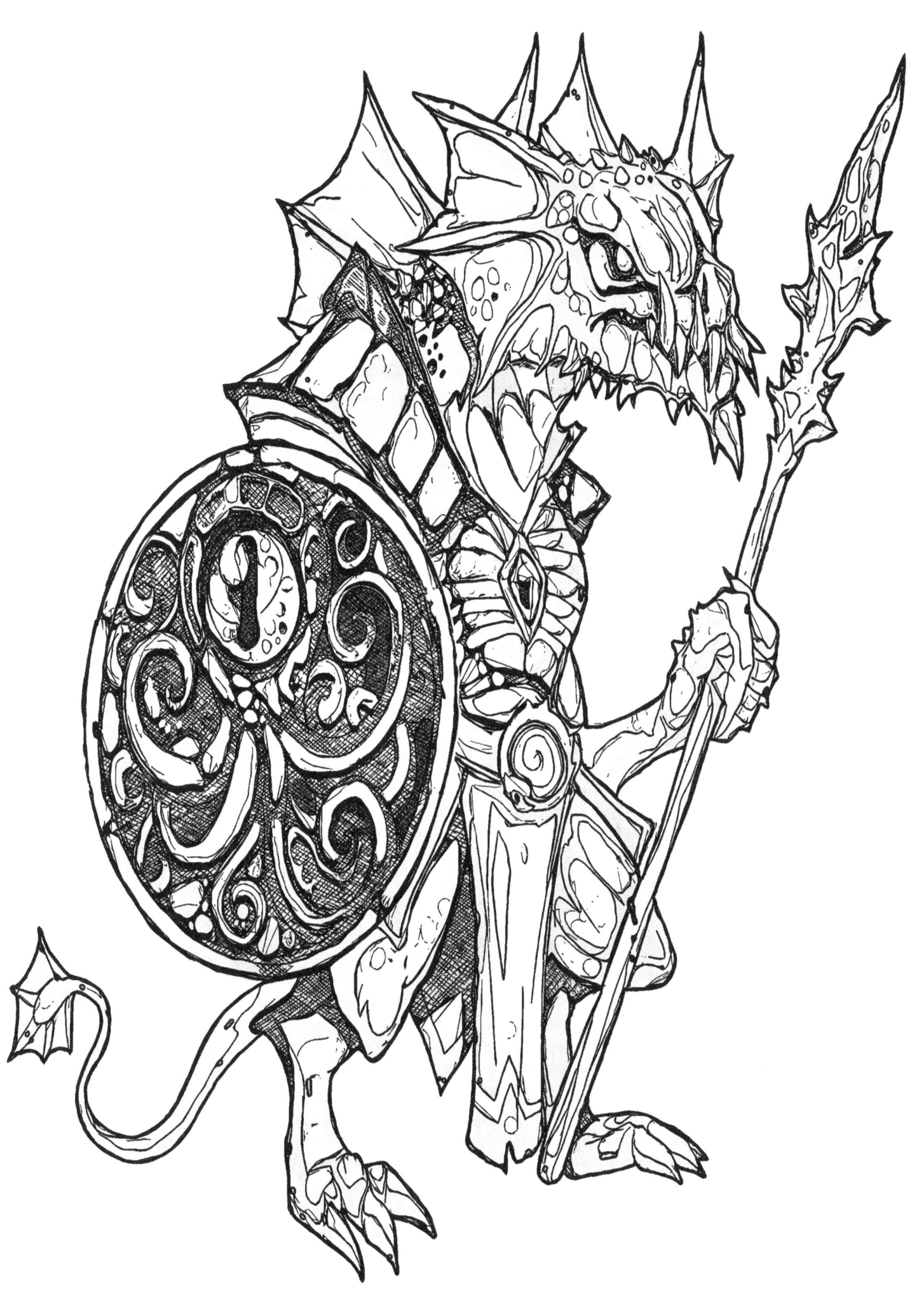

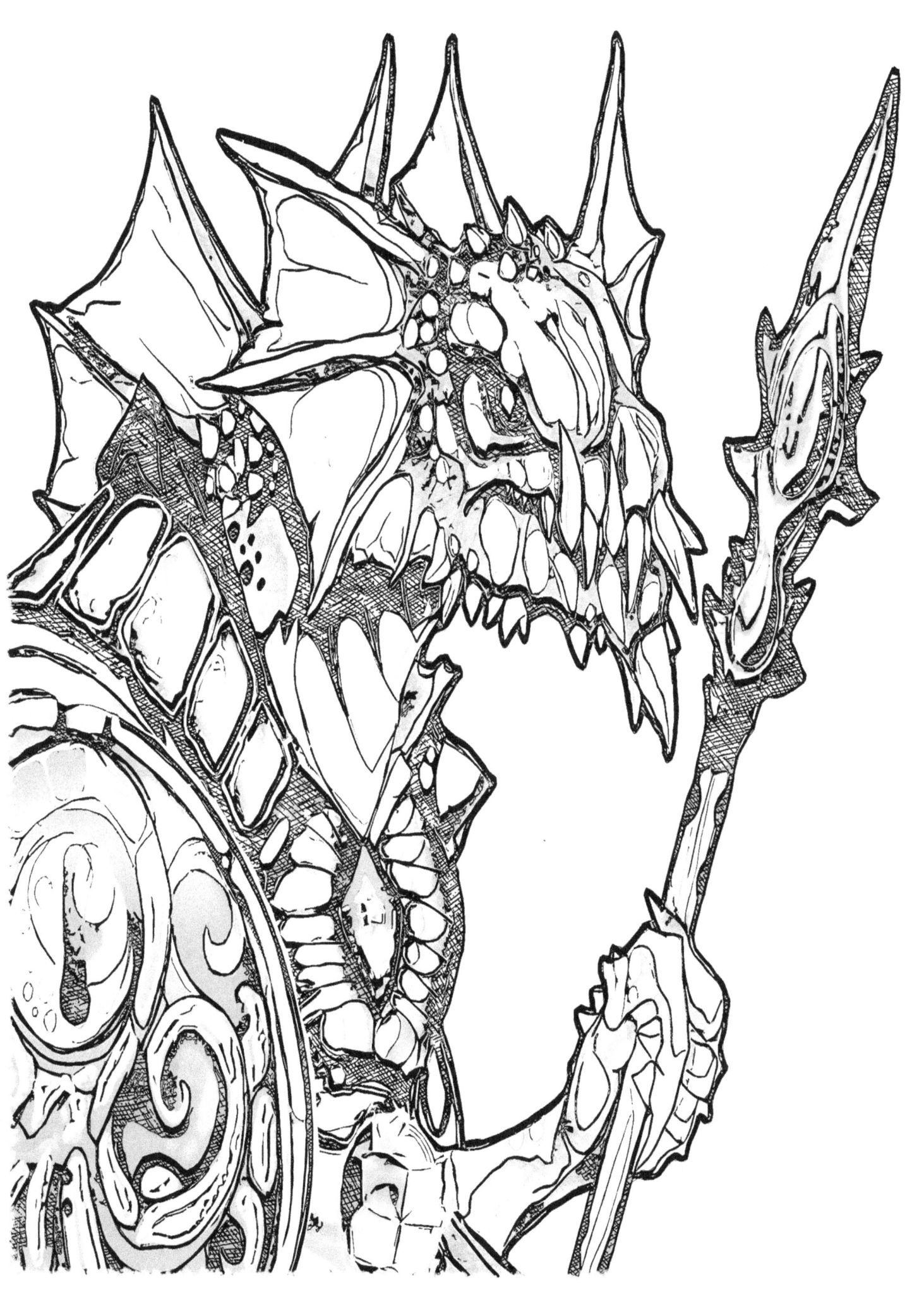

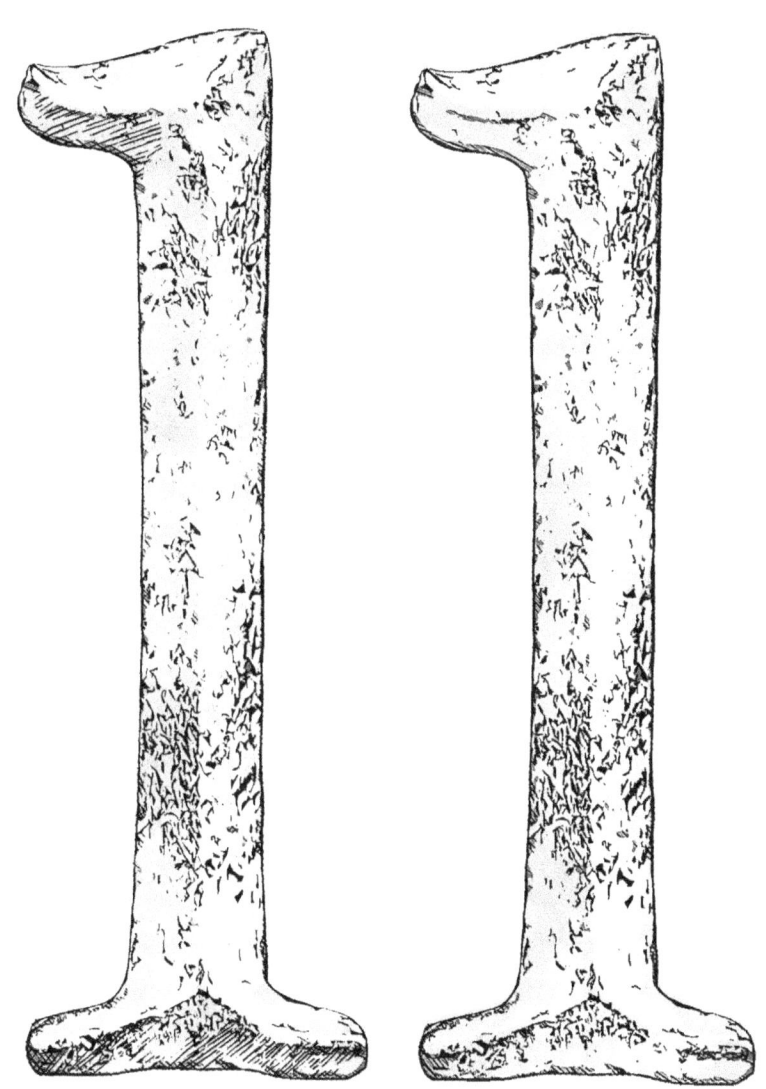

PLANISARIA HURRICANE

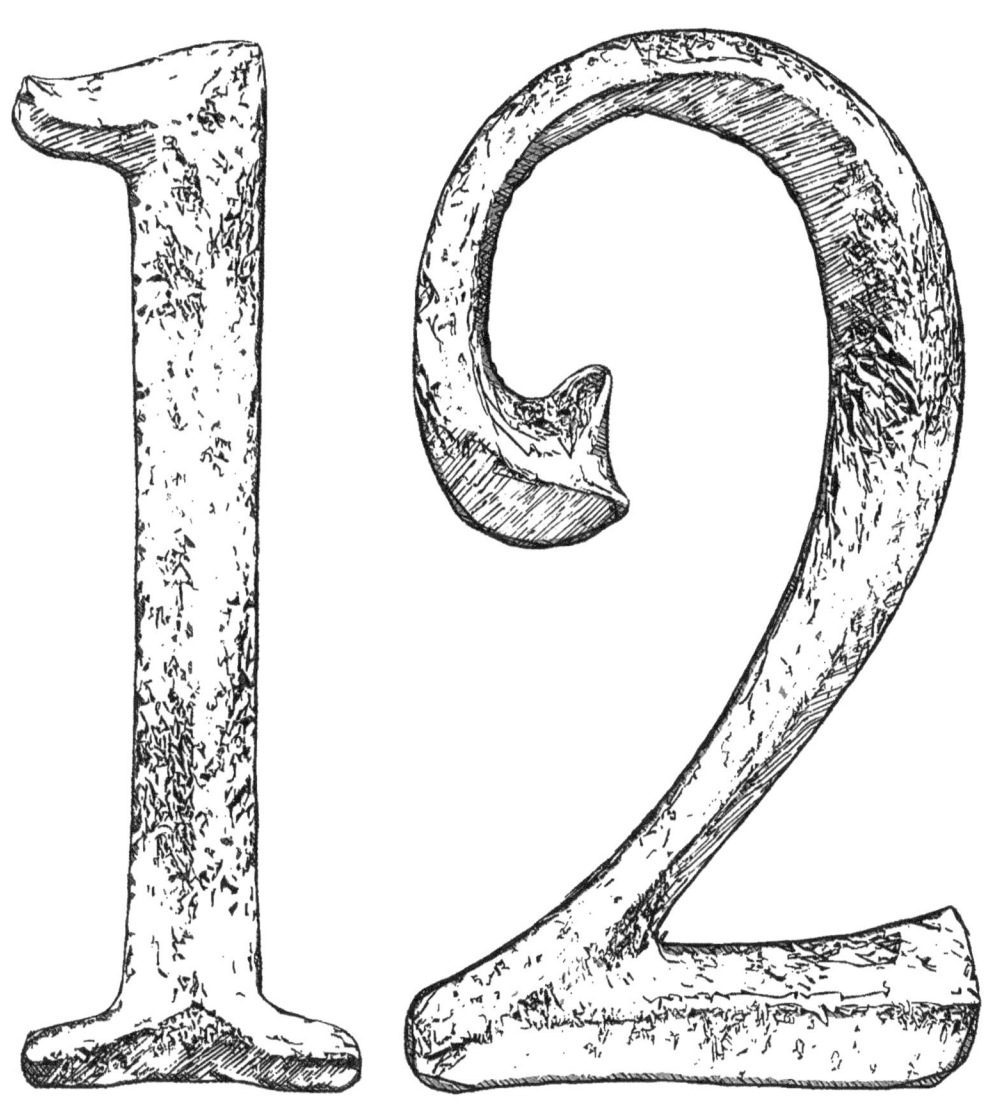

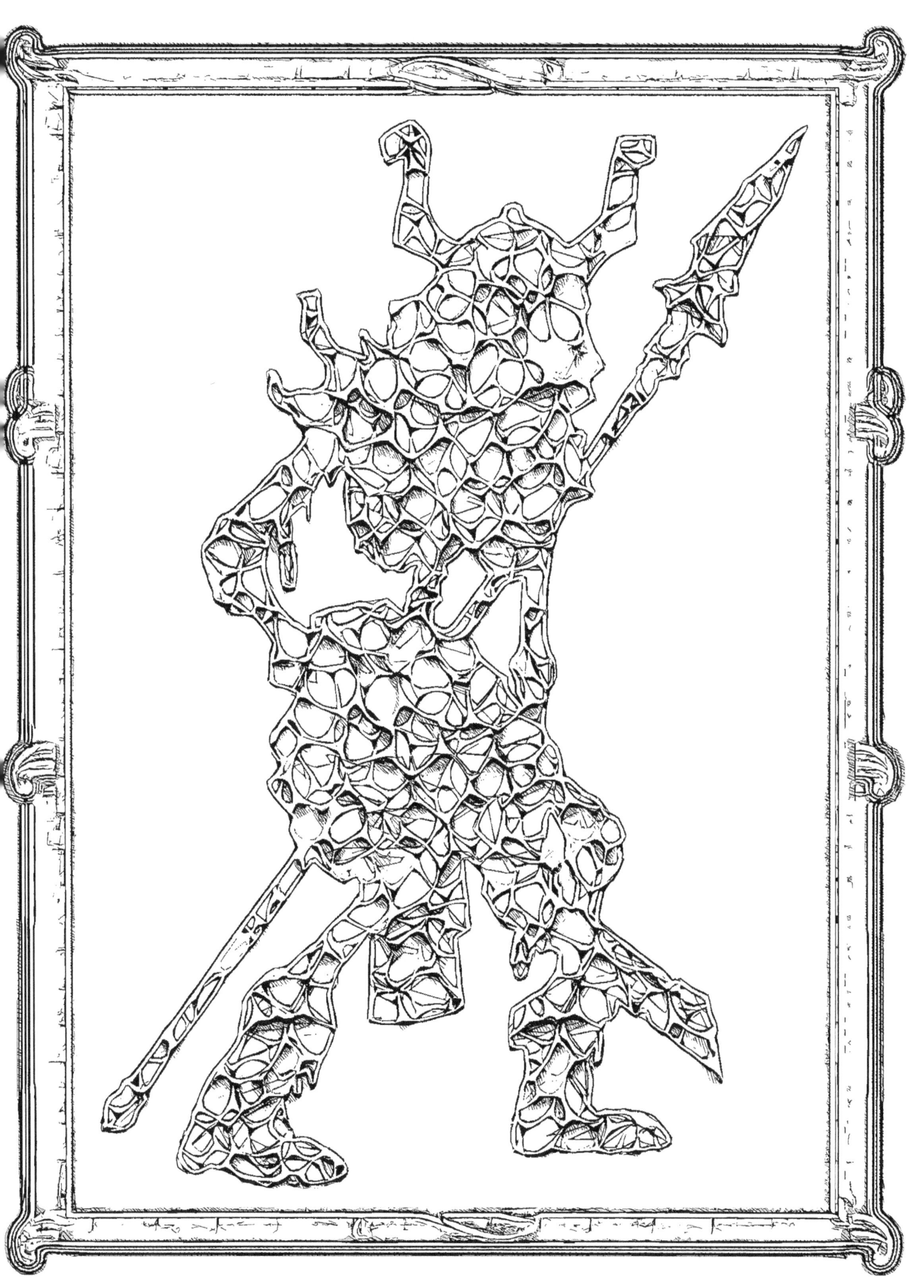

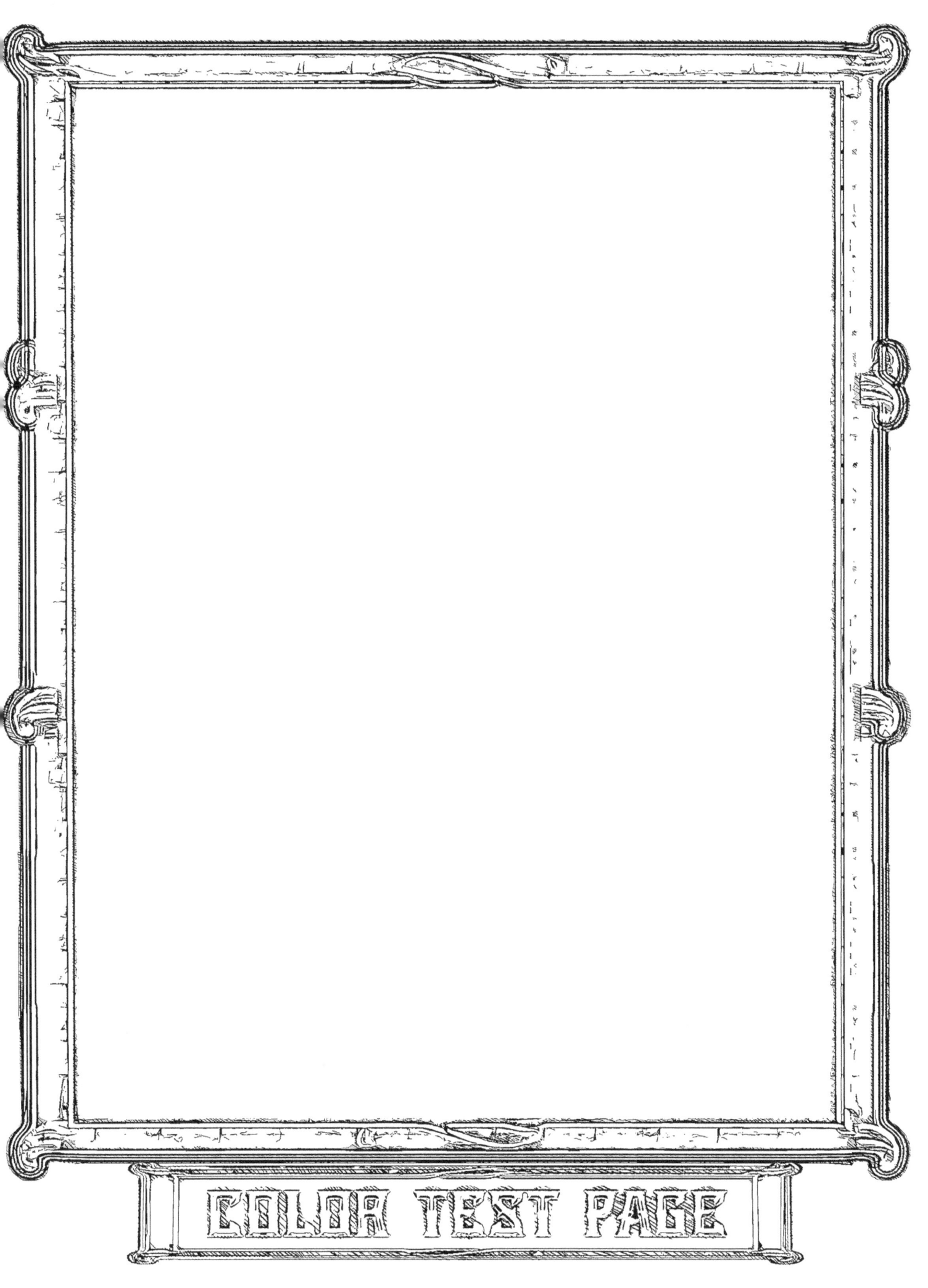

COLOR TEST PAGE

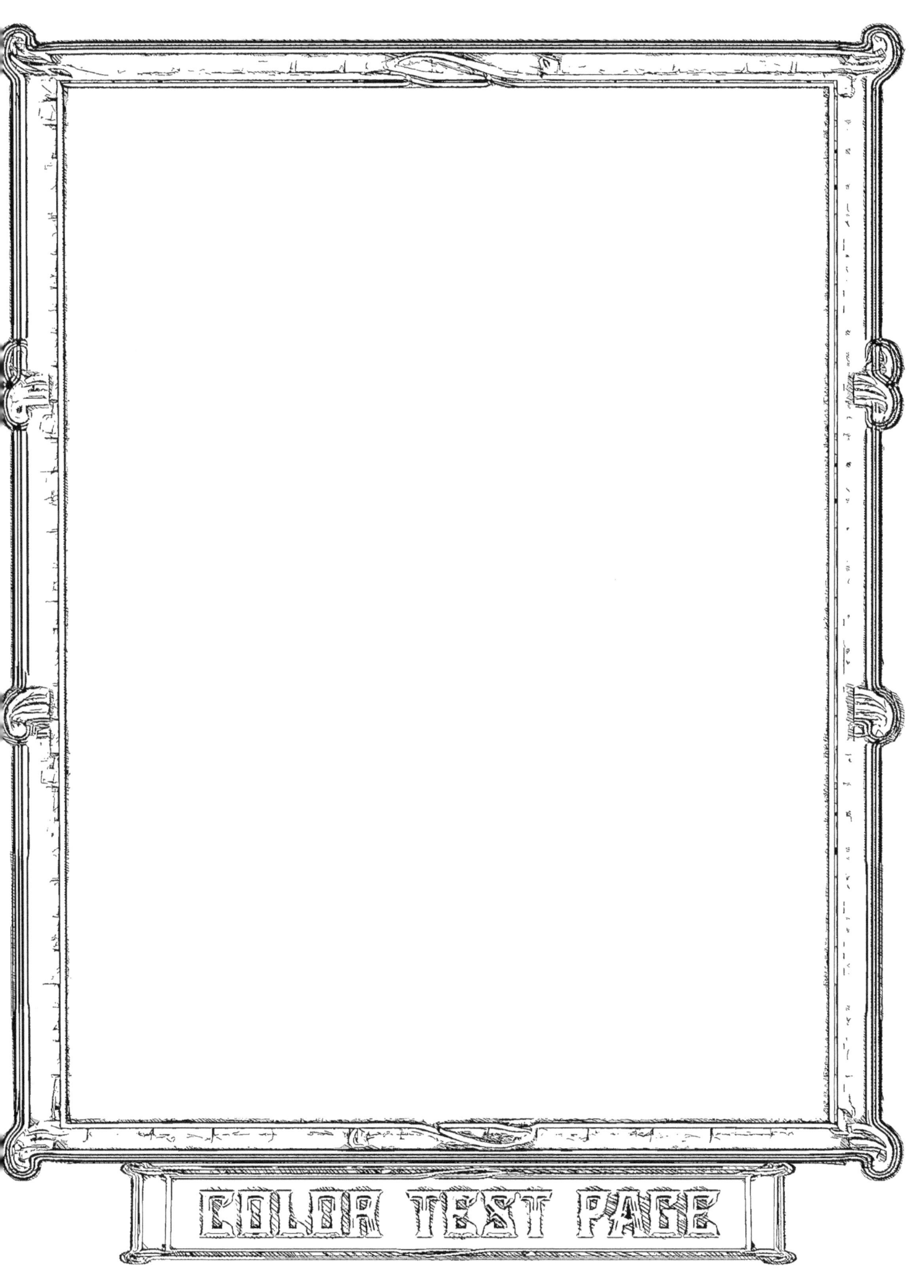

COLOR TEST PAGE

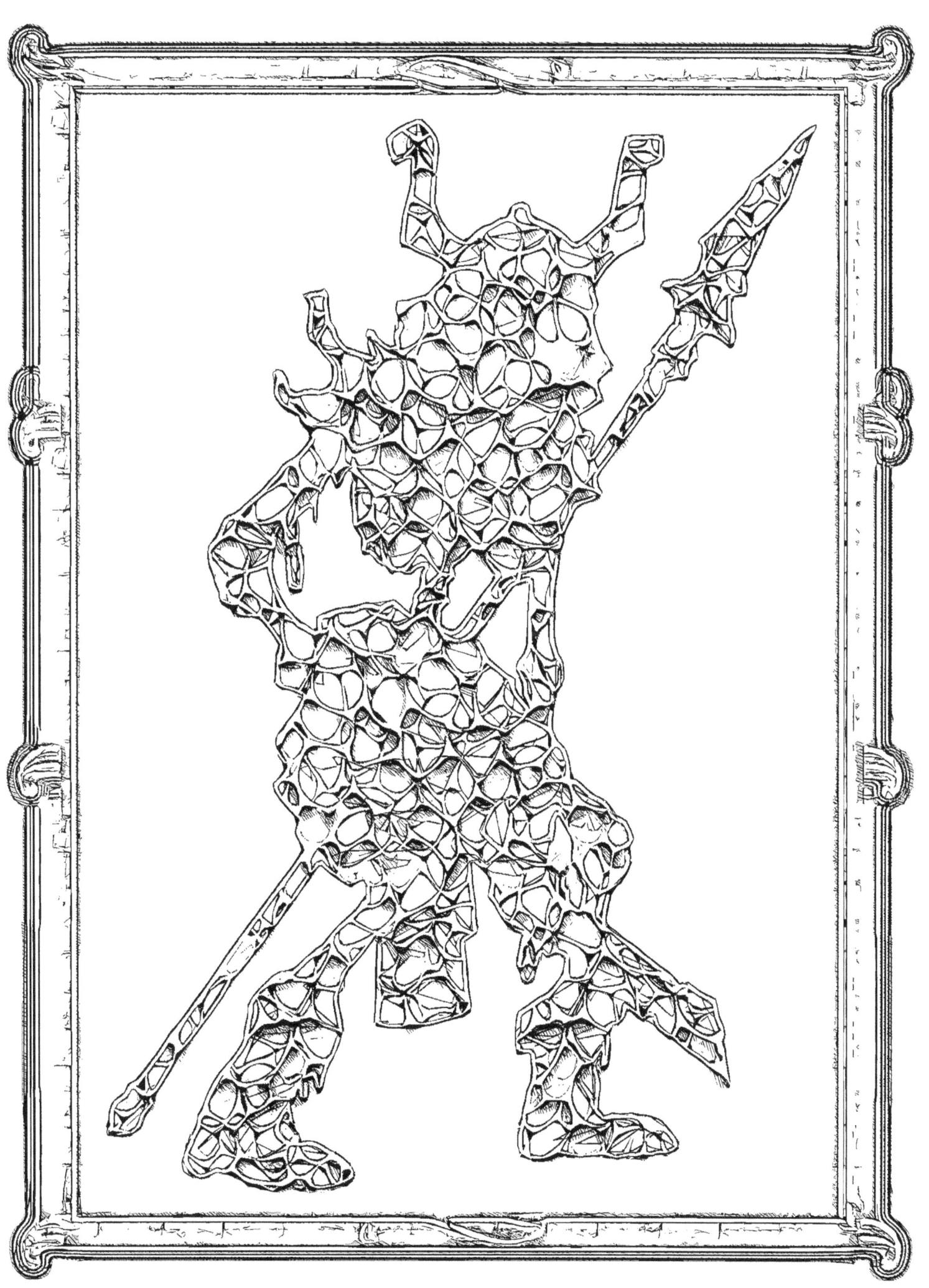

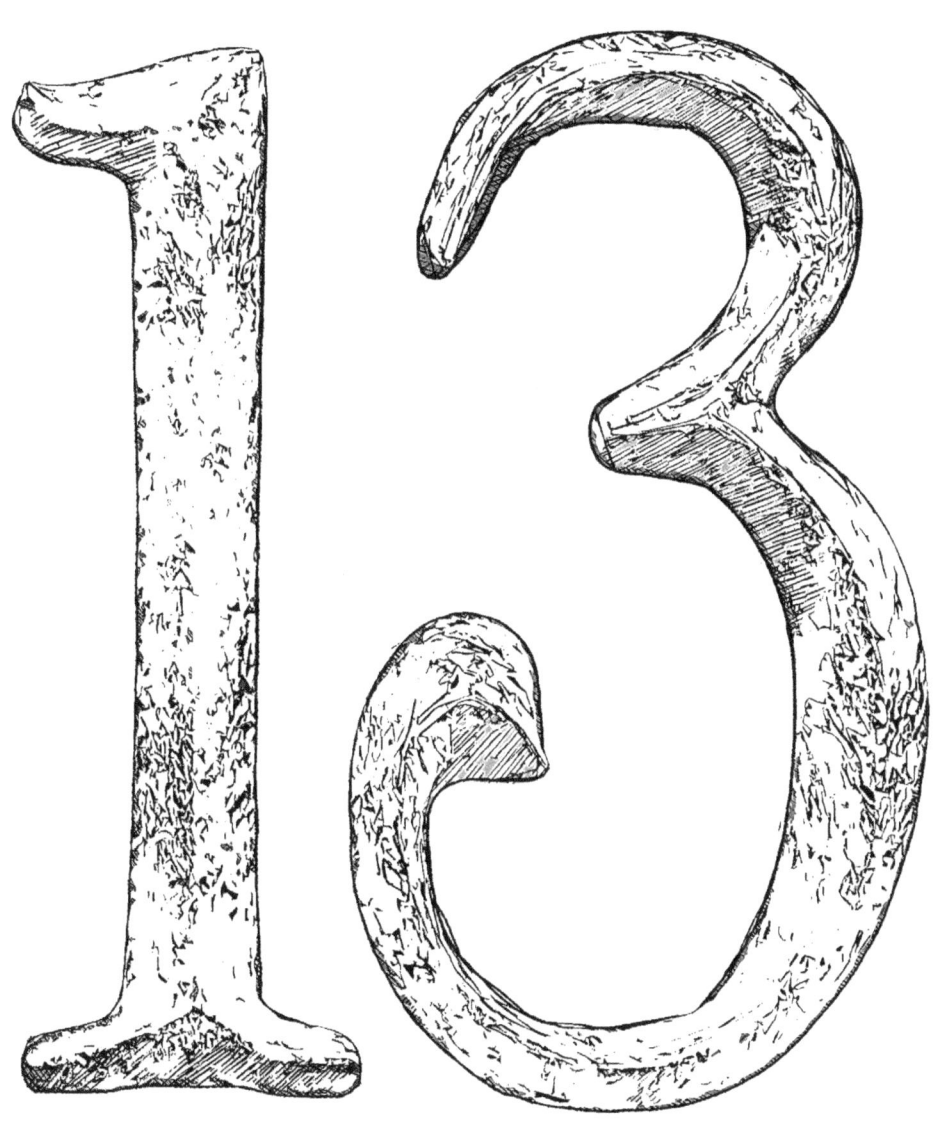

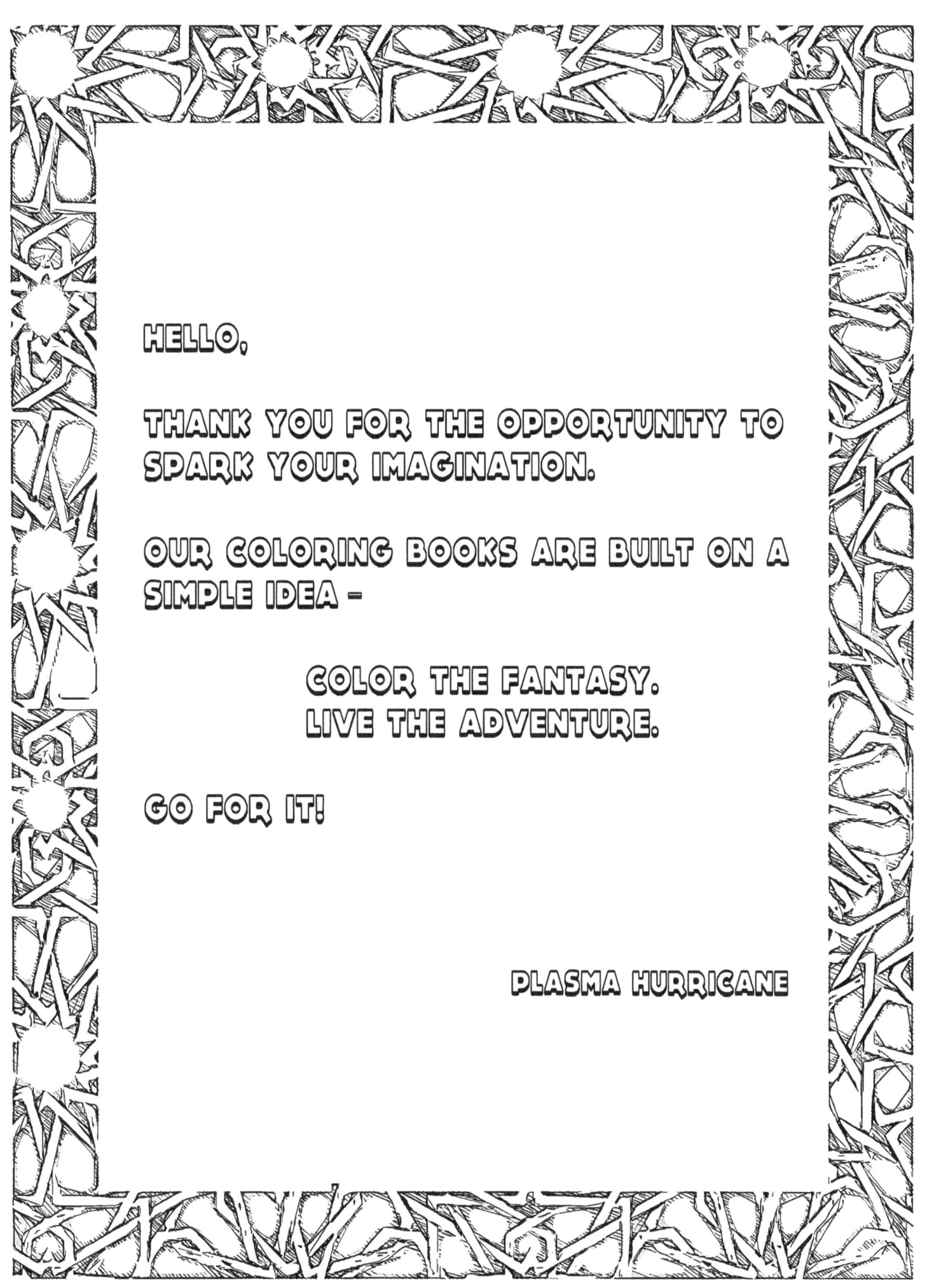

HELLO,

THANK YOU FOR THE OPPORTUNITY TO SPARK YOUR IMAGINATION.

OUR COLORING BOOKS ARE BUILT ON A SIMPLE IDEA –

COLOR THE FANTASY.
LIVE THE ADVENTURE.

GO FOR IT!

PLASMA HURRICANE

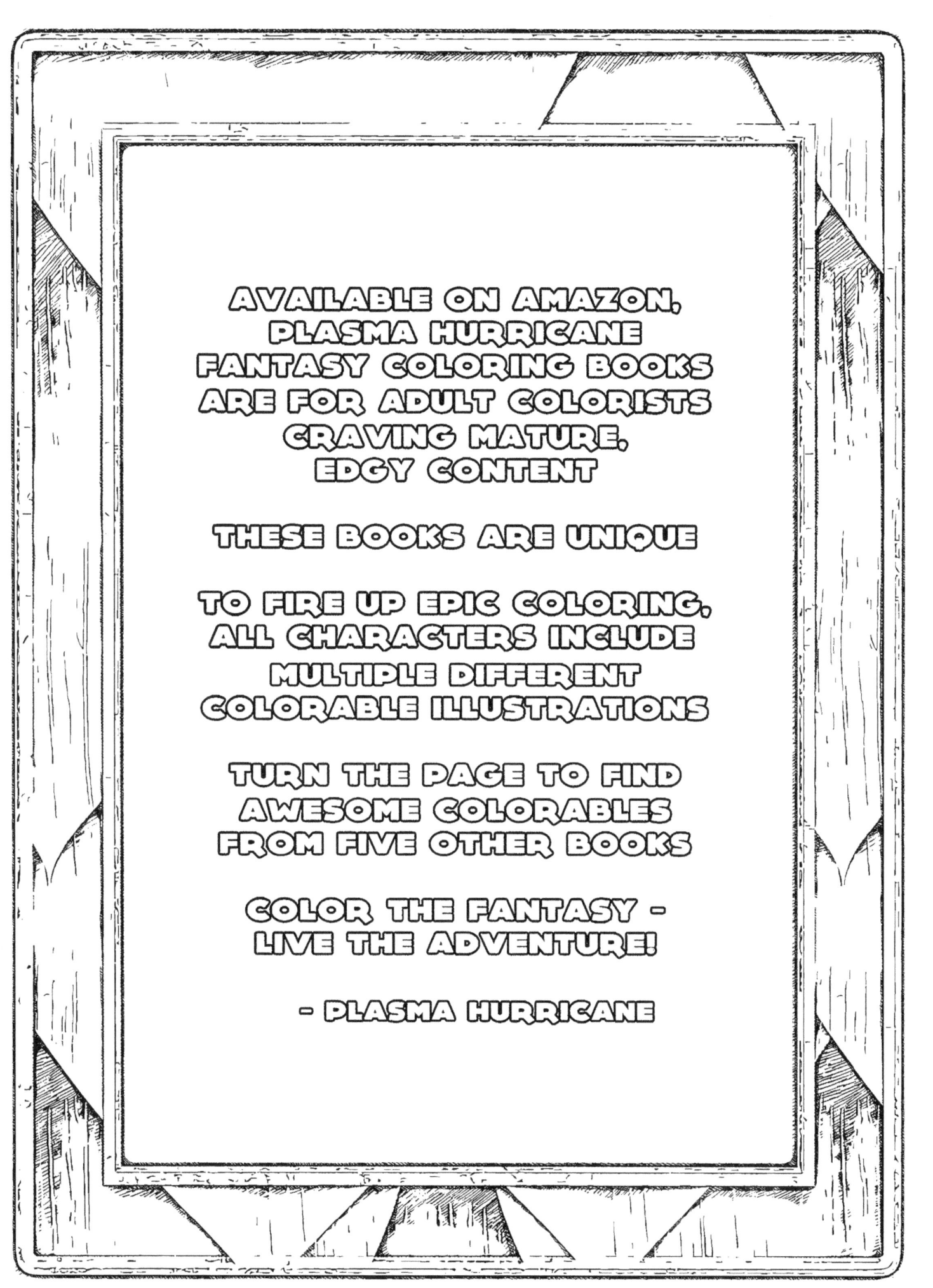

AVAILABLE ON AMAZON,
PLASMA HURRICANE
FANTASY COLORING BOOKS
ARE FOR ADULT COLORISTS
CRAVING MATURE,
EDGY CONTENT

THESE BOOKS ARE UNIQUE

TO FIRE UP EPIC COLORING,
ALL CHARACTERS INCLUDE
MULTIPLE DIFFERENT
COLORABLE ILLUSTRATIONS

TURN THE PAGE TO FIND
AWESOME COLORABLES
FROM FIVE OTHER BOOKS

COLOR THE FANTASY –
LIVE THE ADVENTURE!

– PLASMA HURRICANE

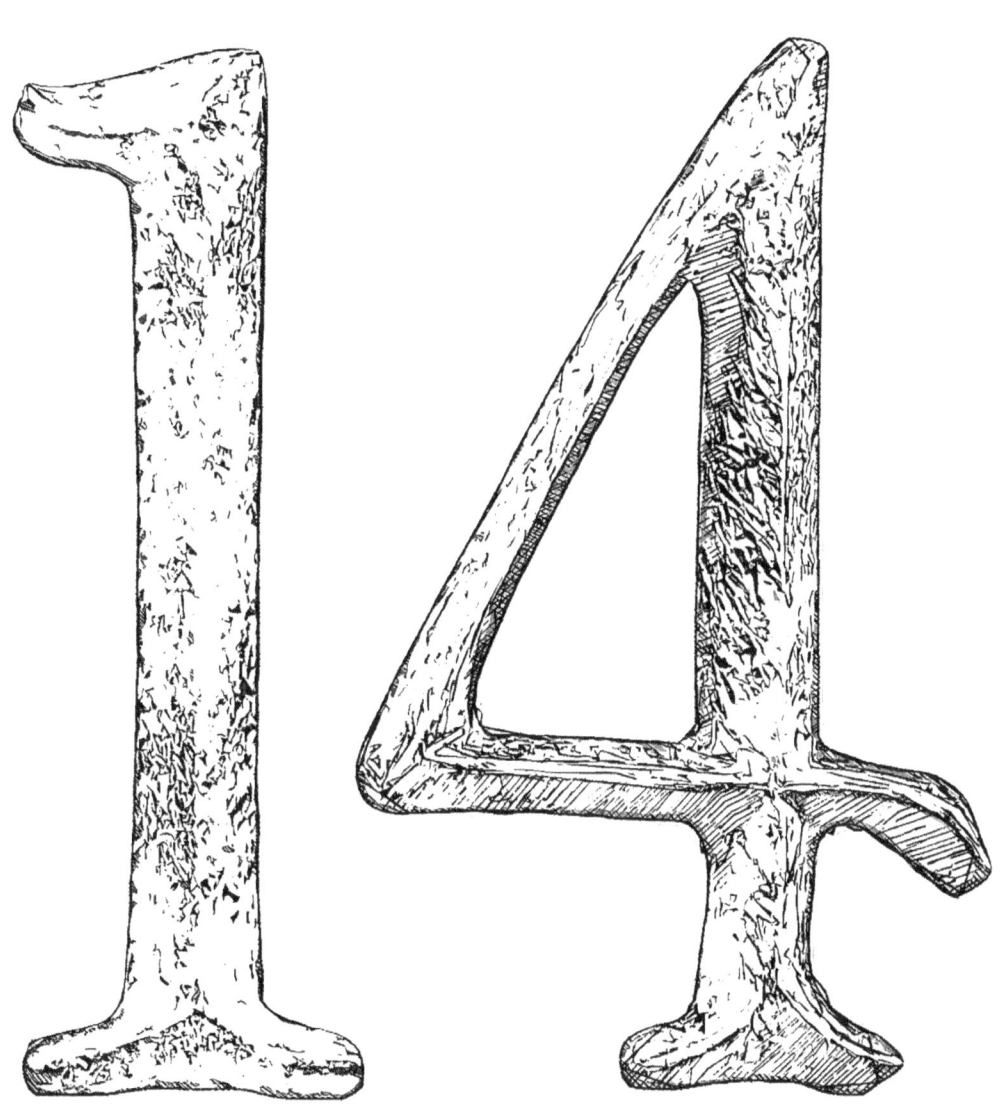

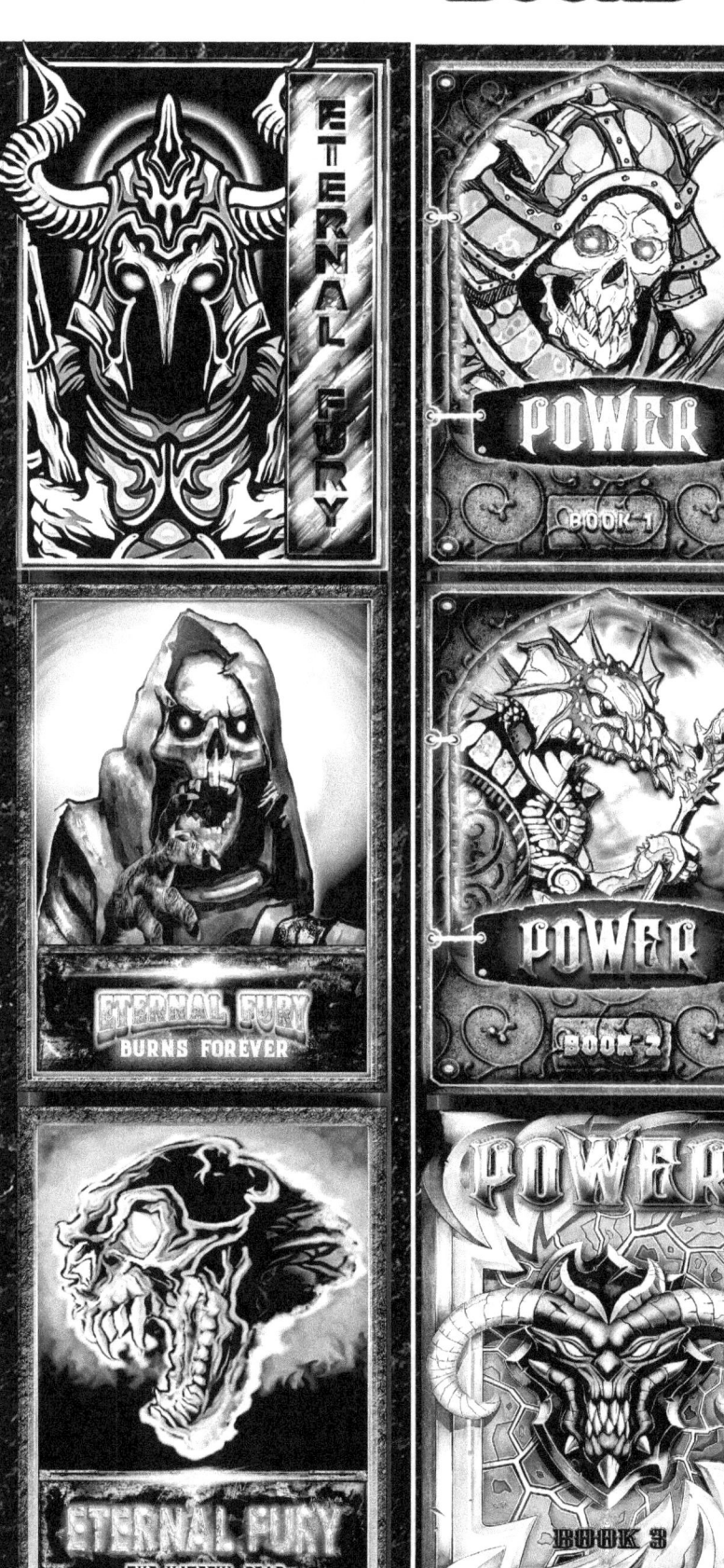

» COMBINES TWO BOOKS:

ETERNAL FURY

ETERNAL FURY: BURNS FOREVER

« COMBINES TWO BOOKS:

POWER: BOOK 1

POWER: BOOK 2

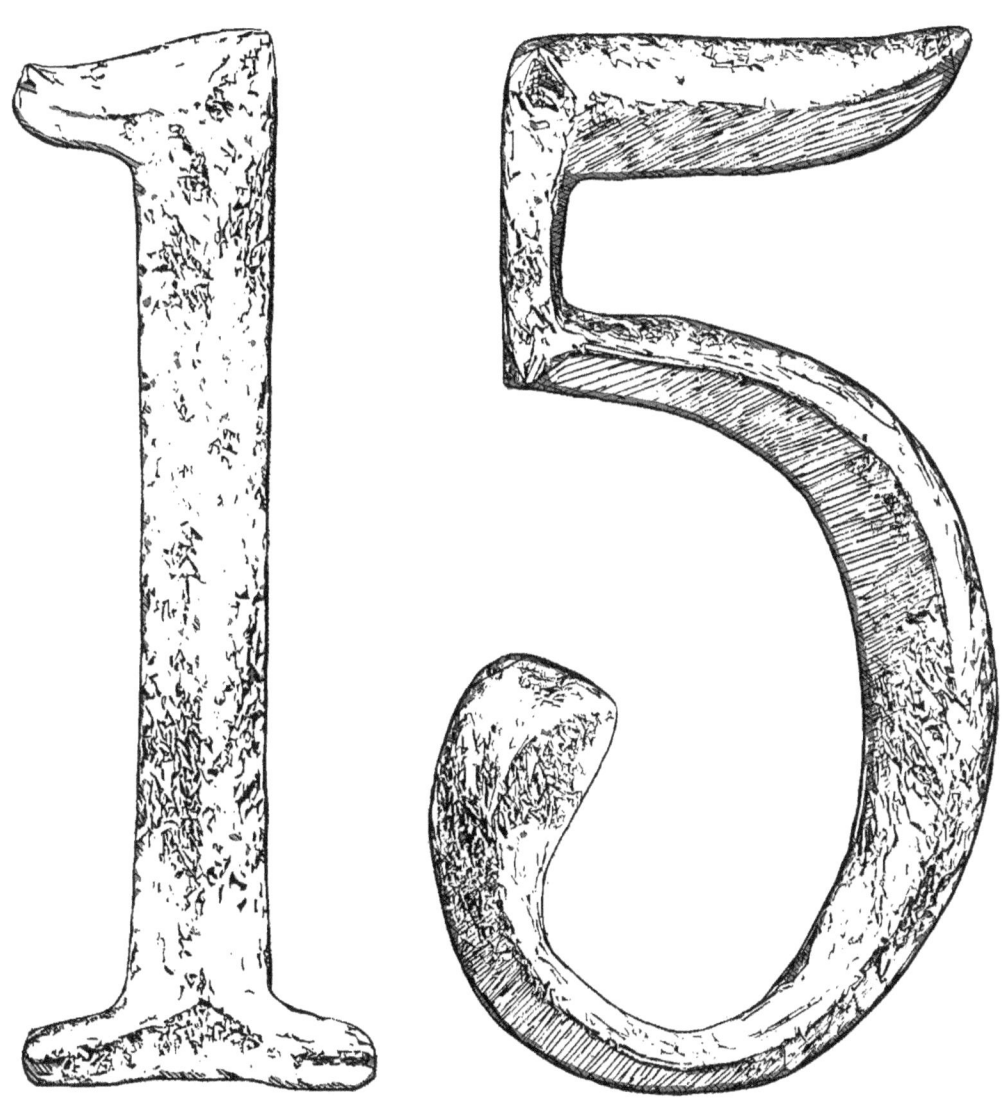

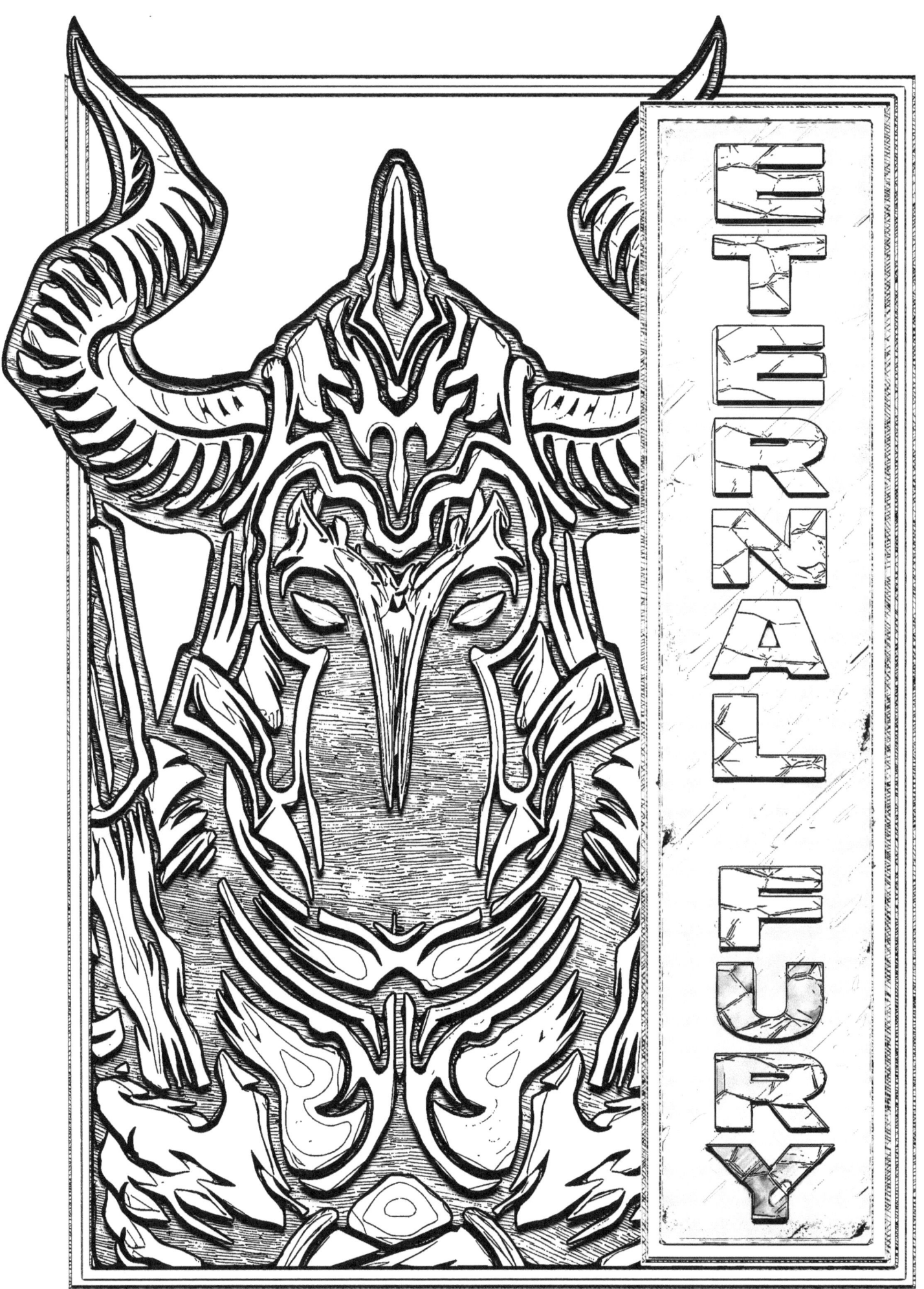

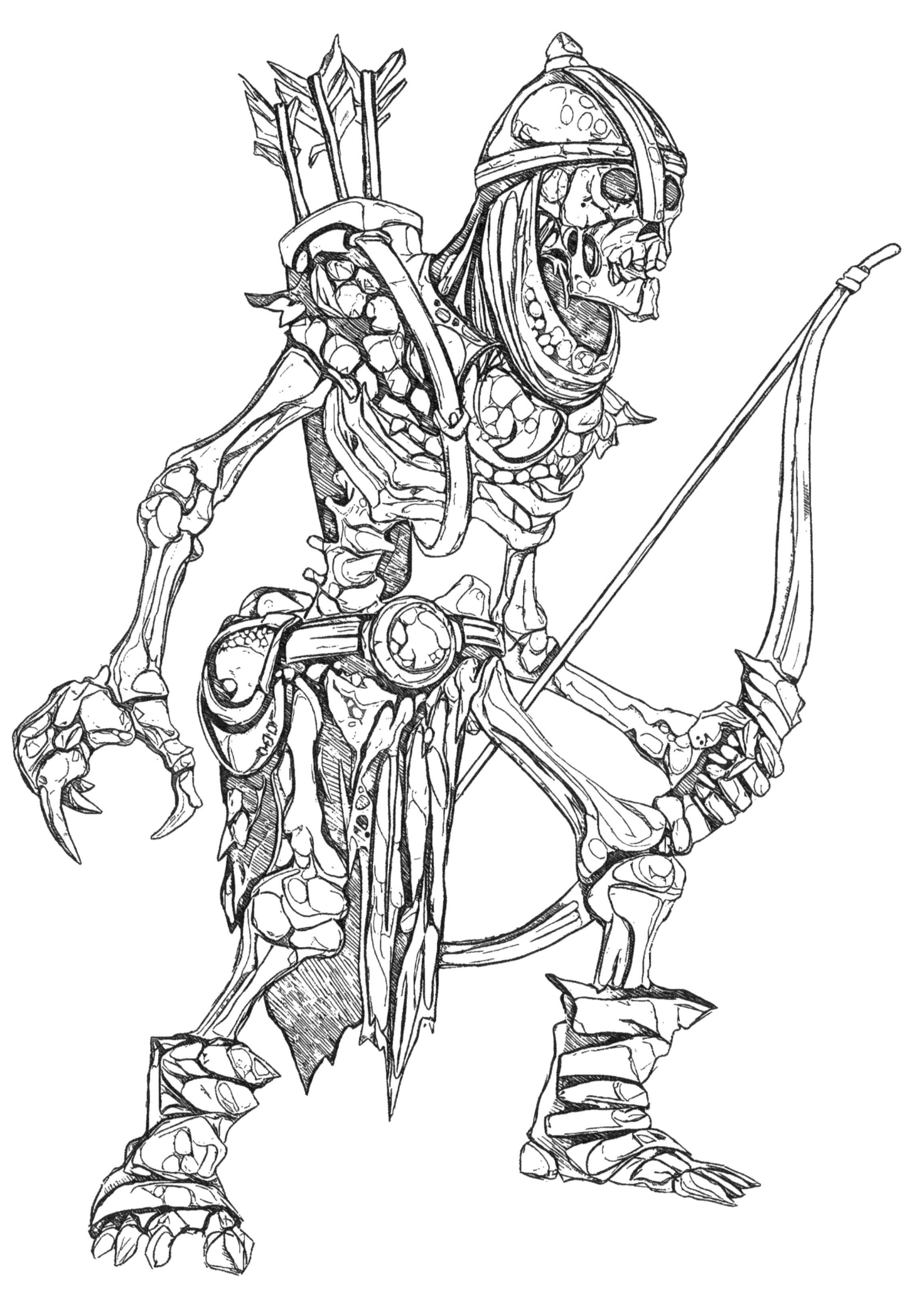

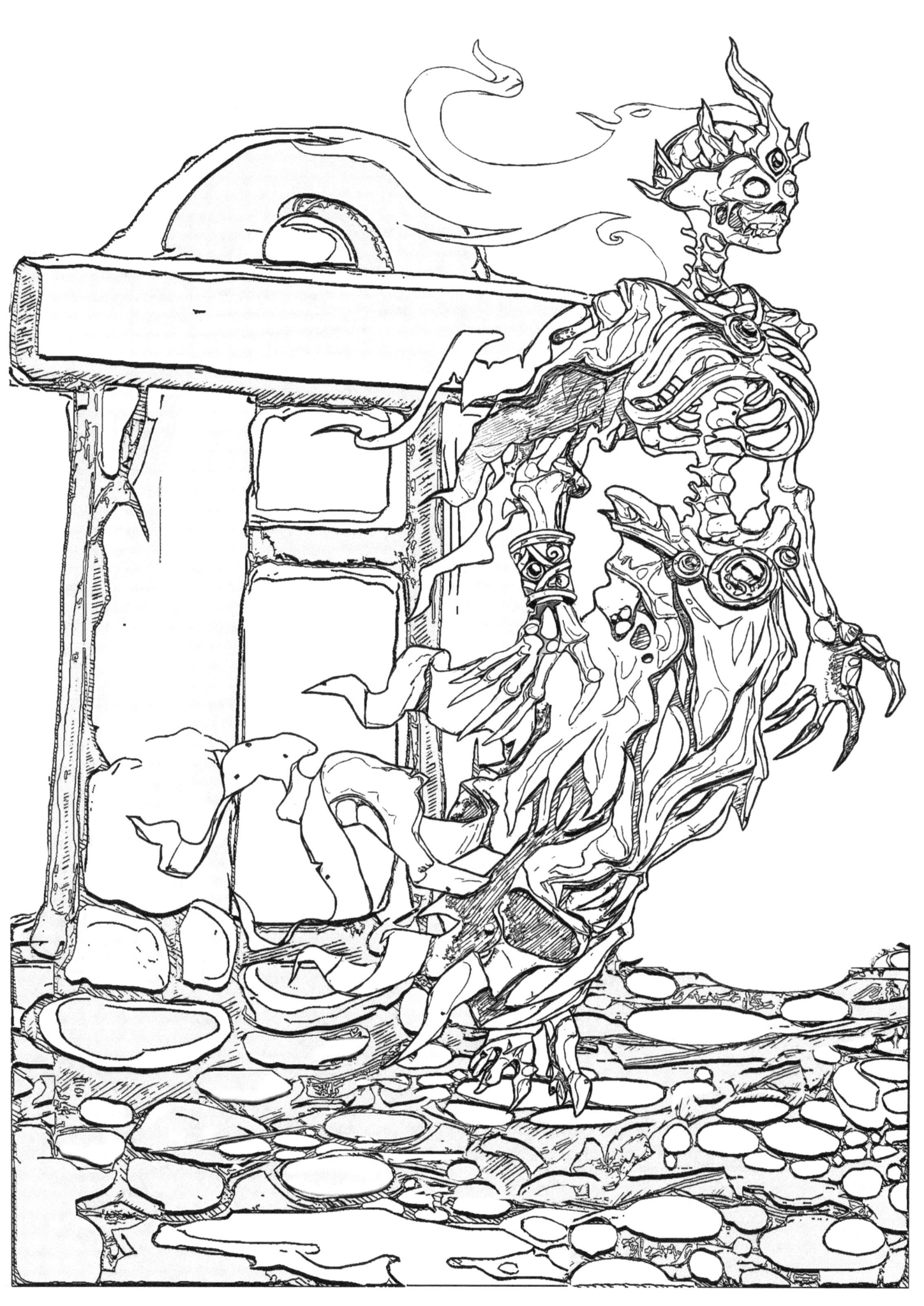

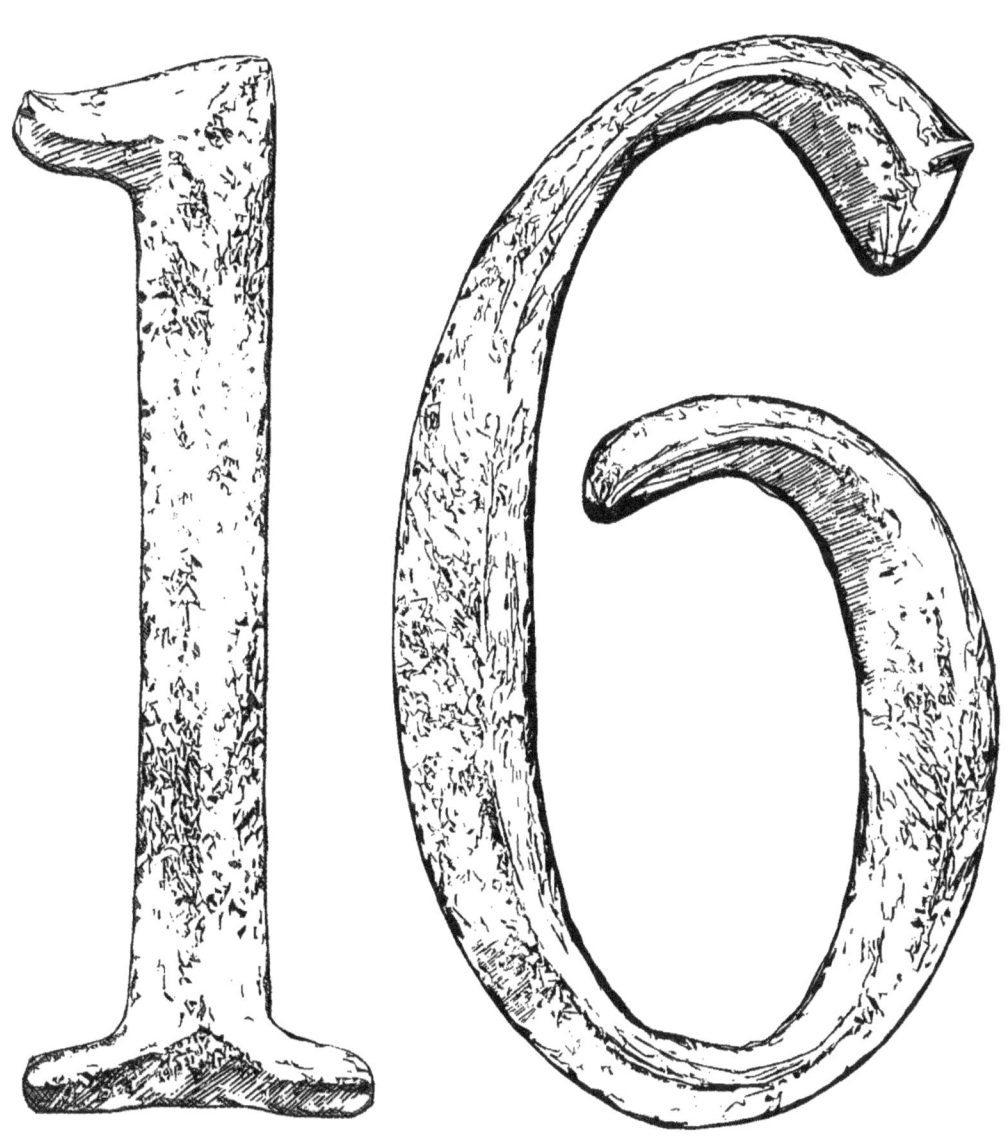

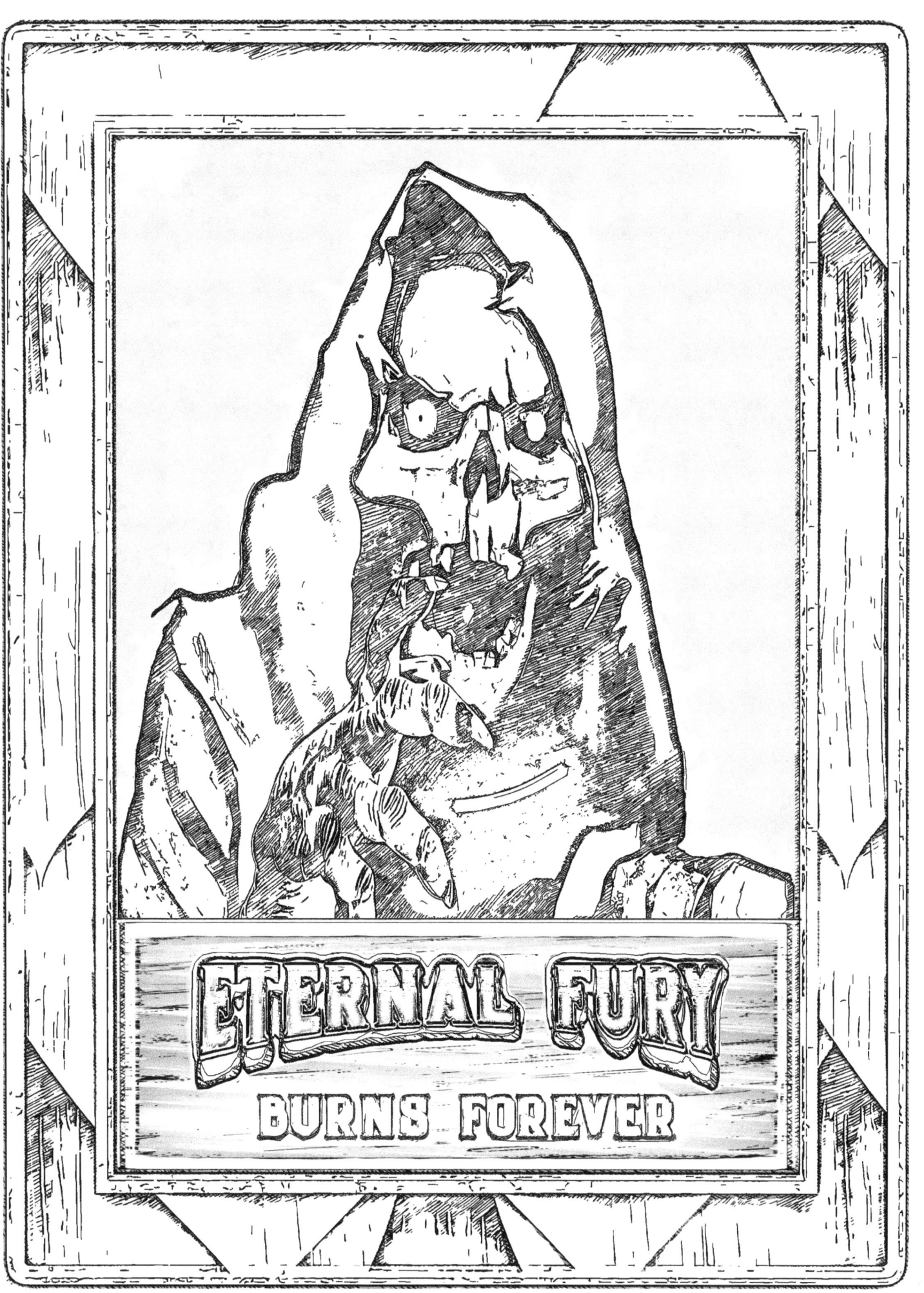

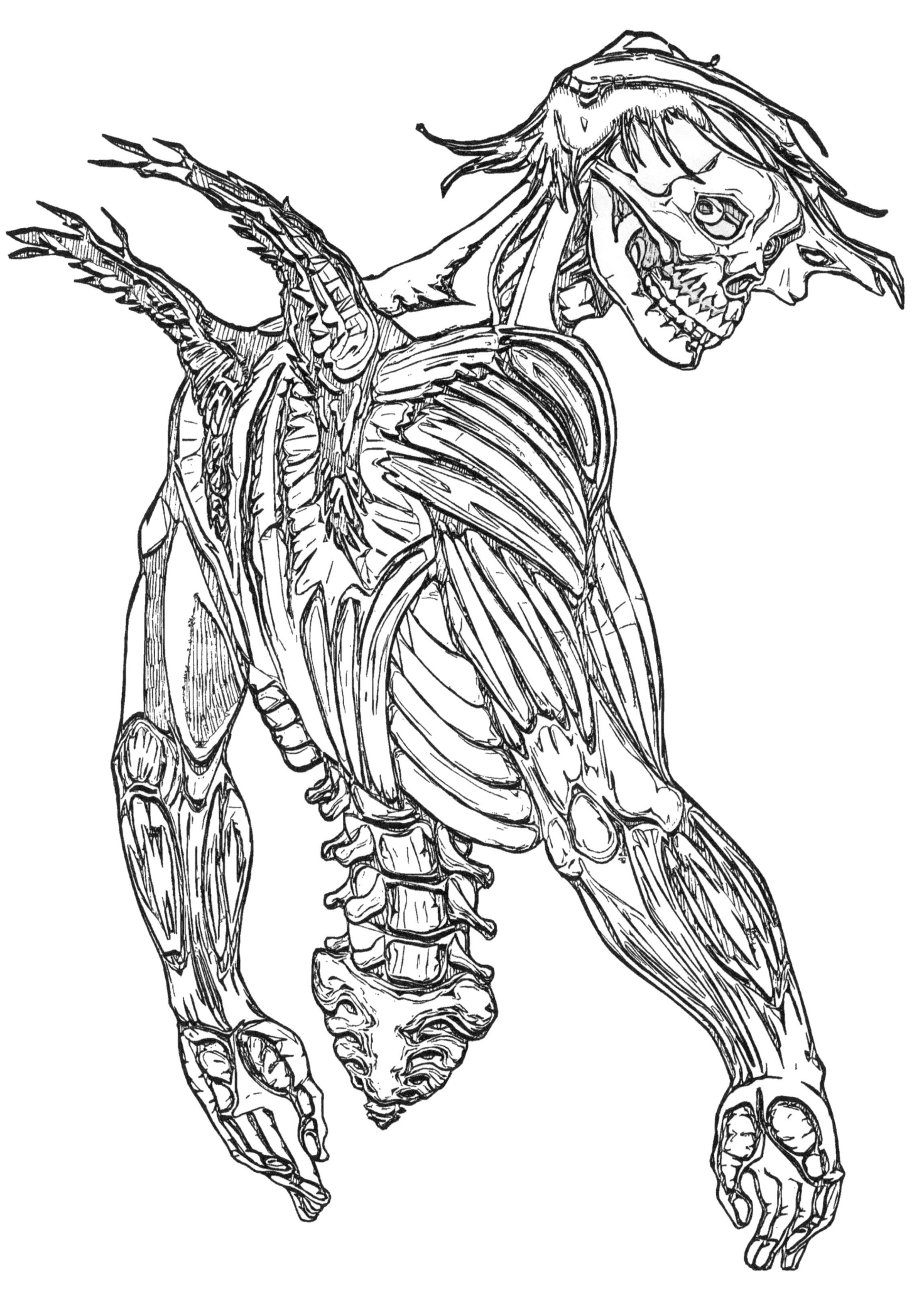

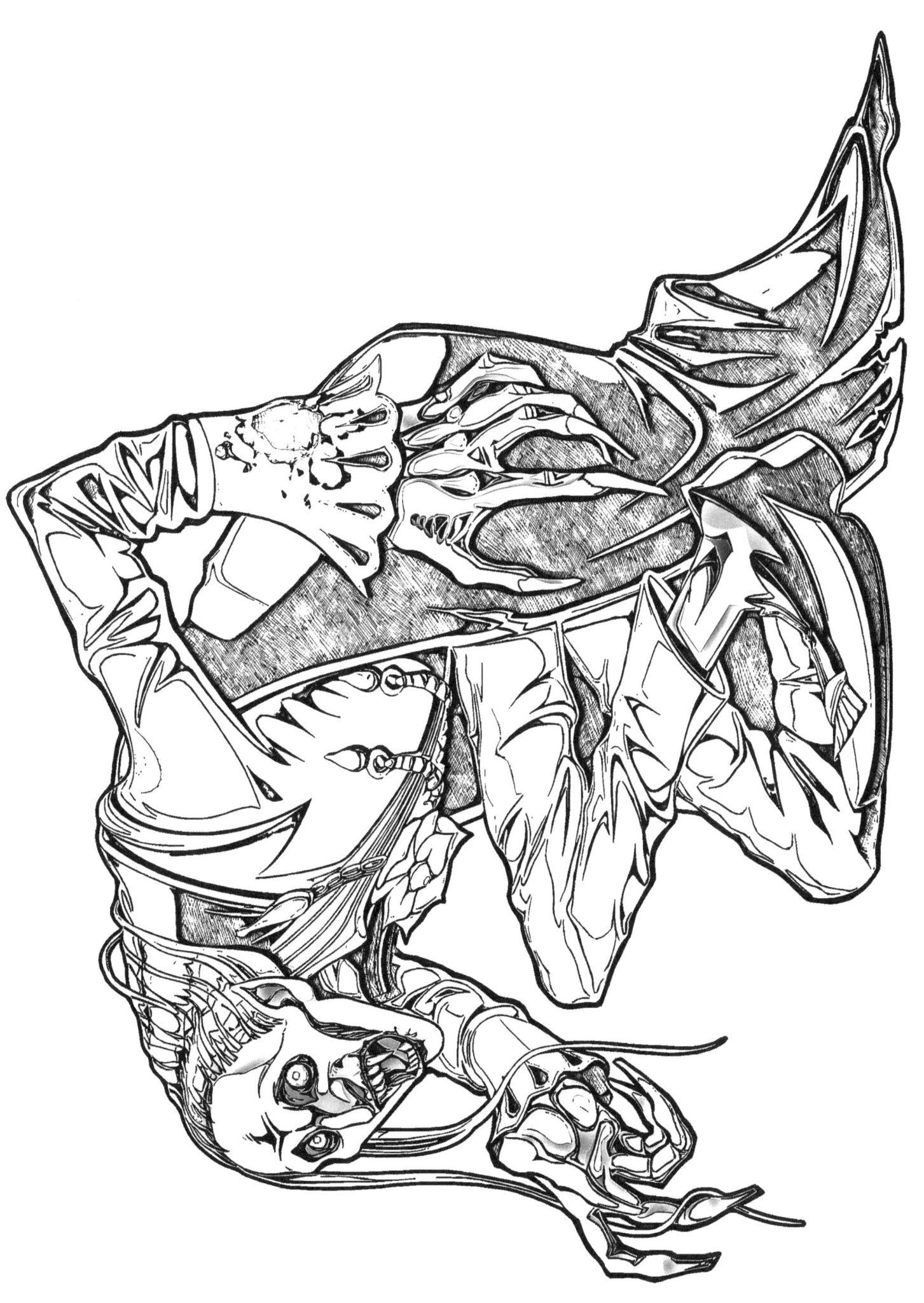

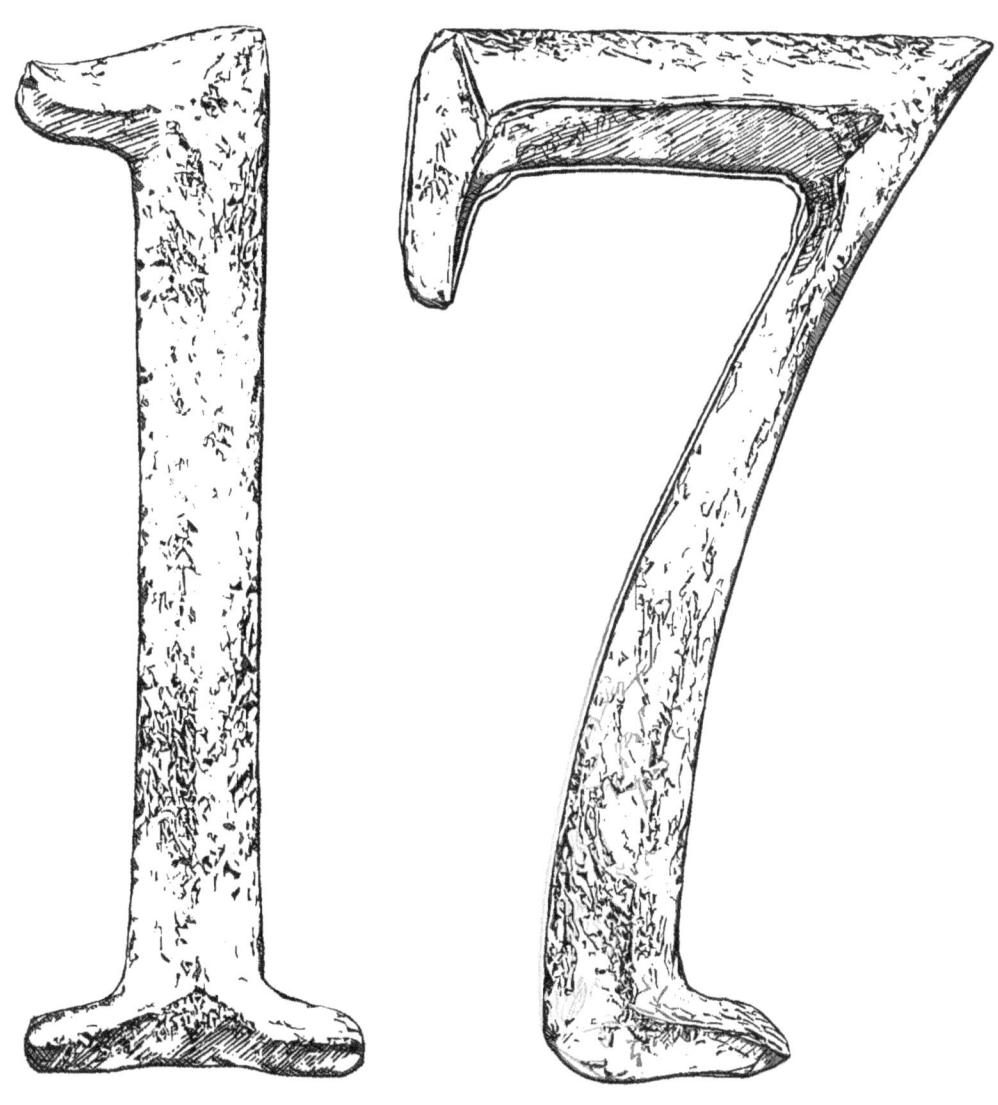

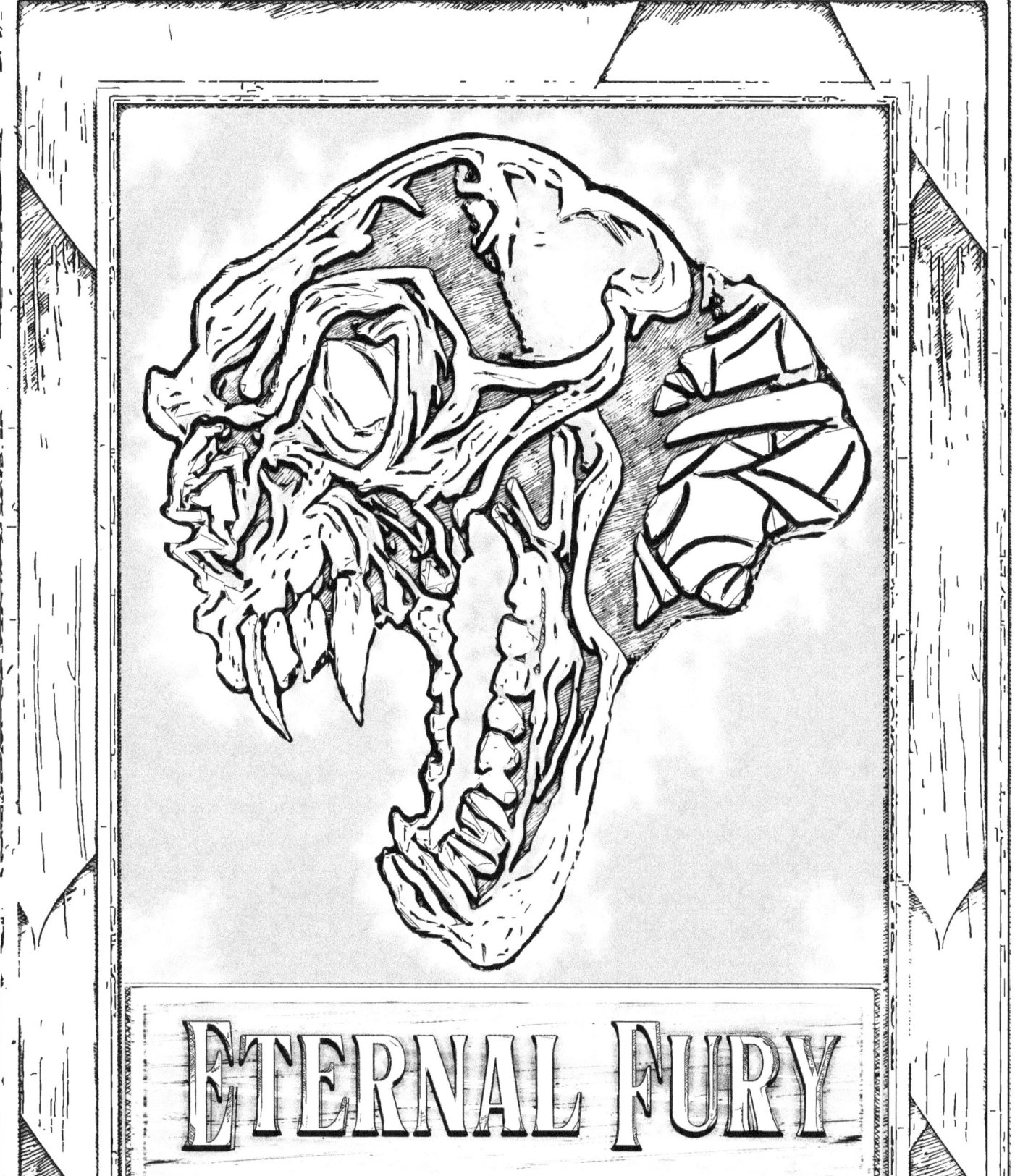

ETERNAL FURY

THE HATEFUL DEAD

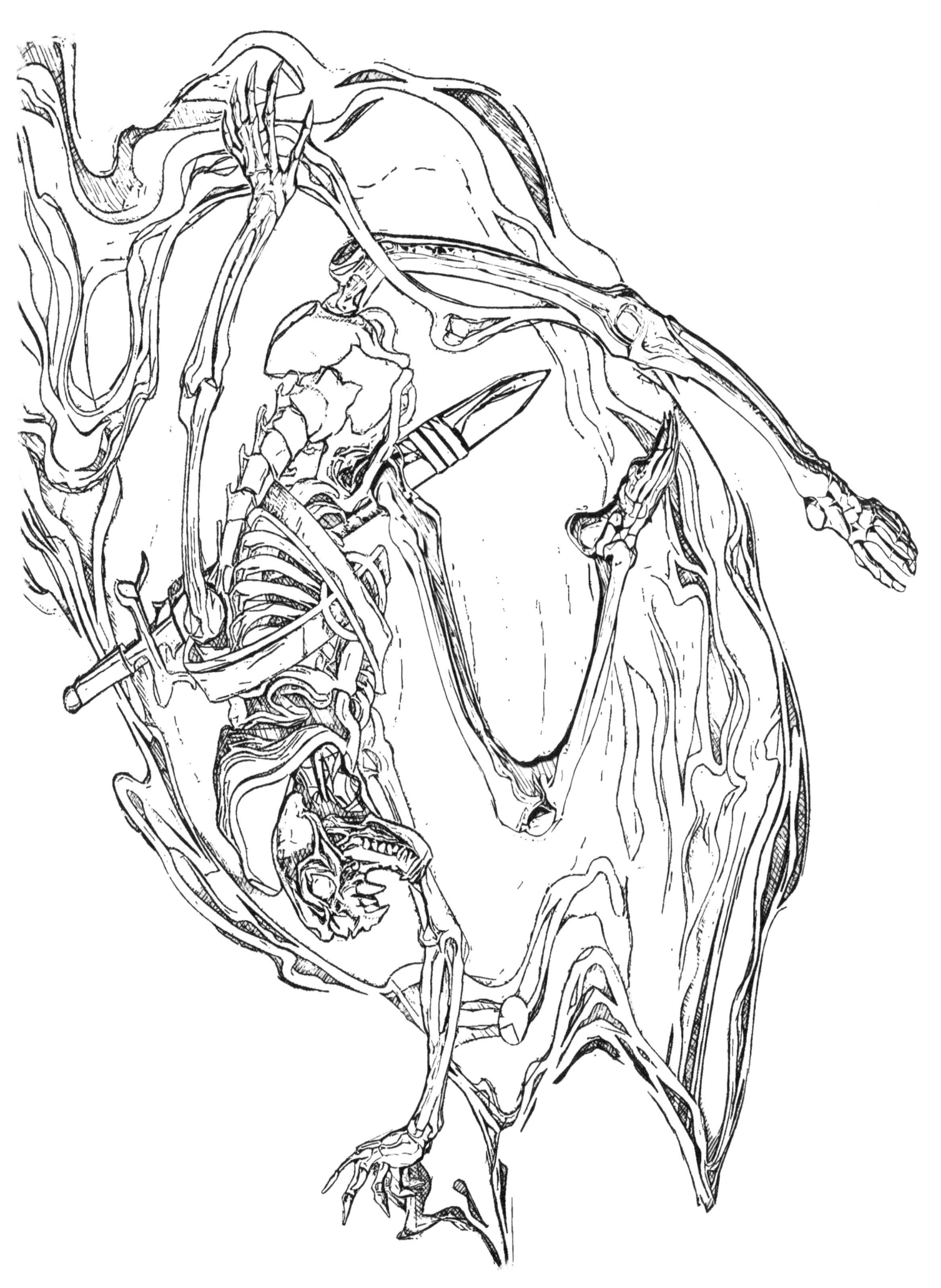

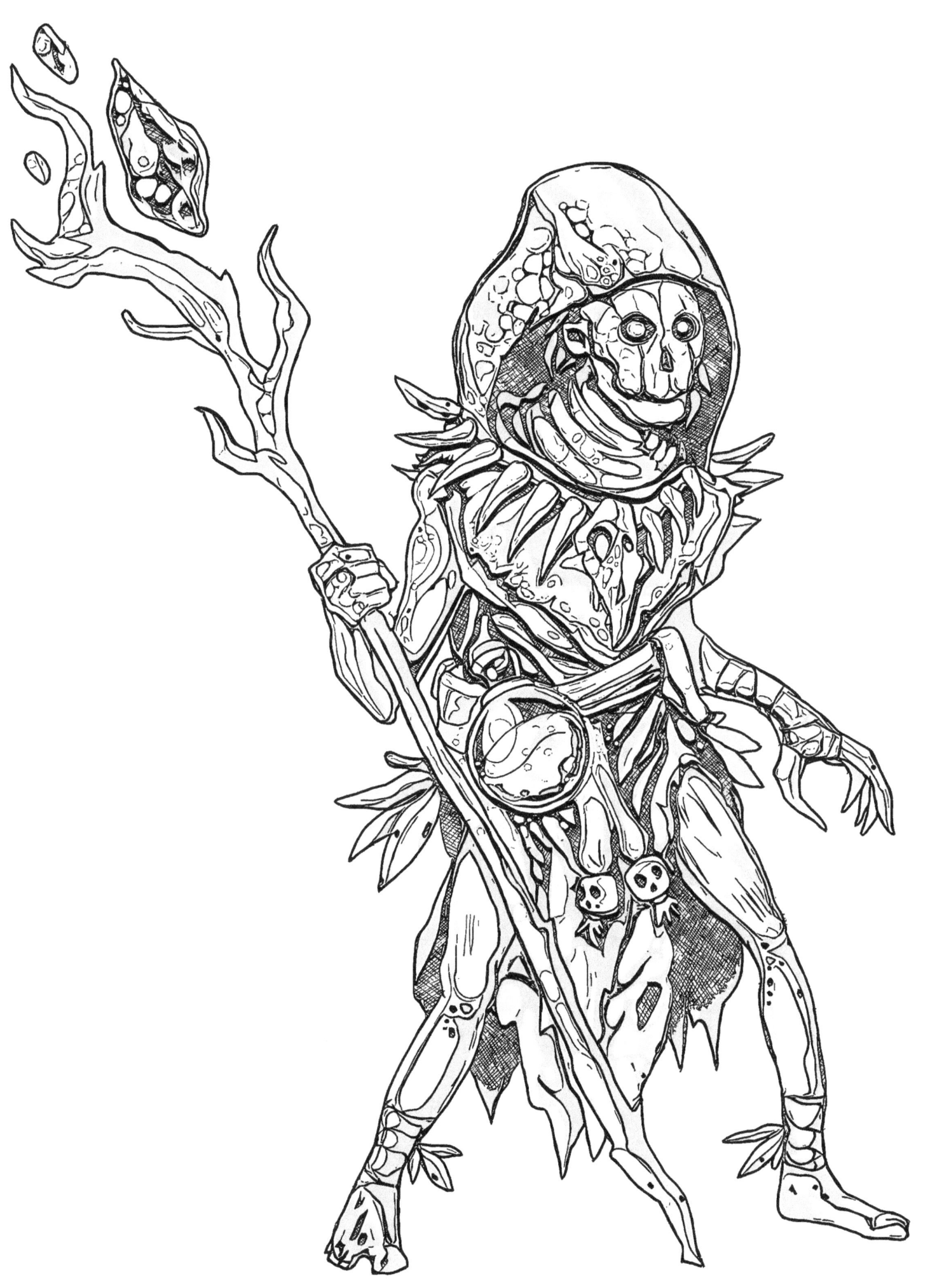

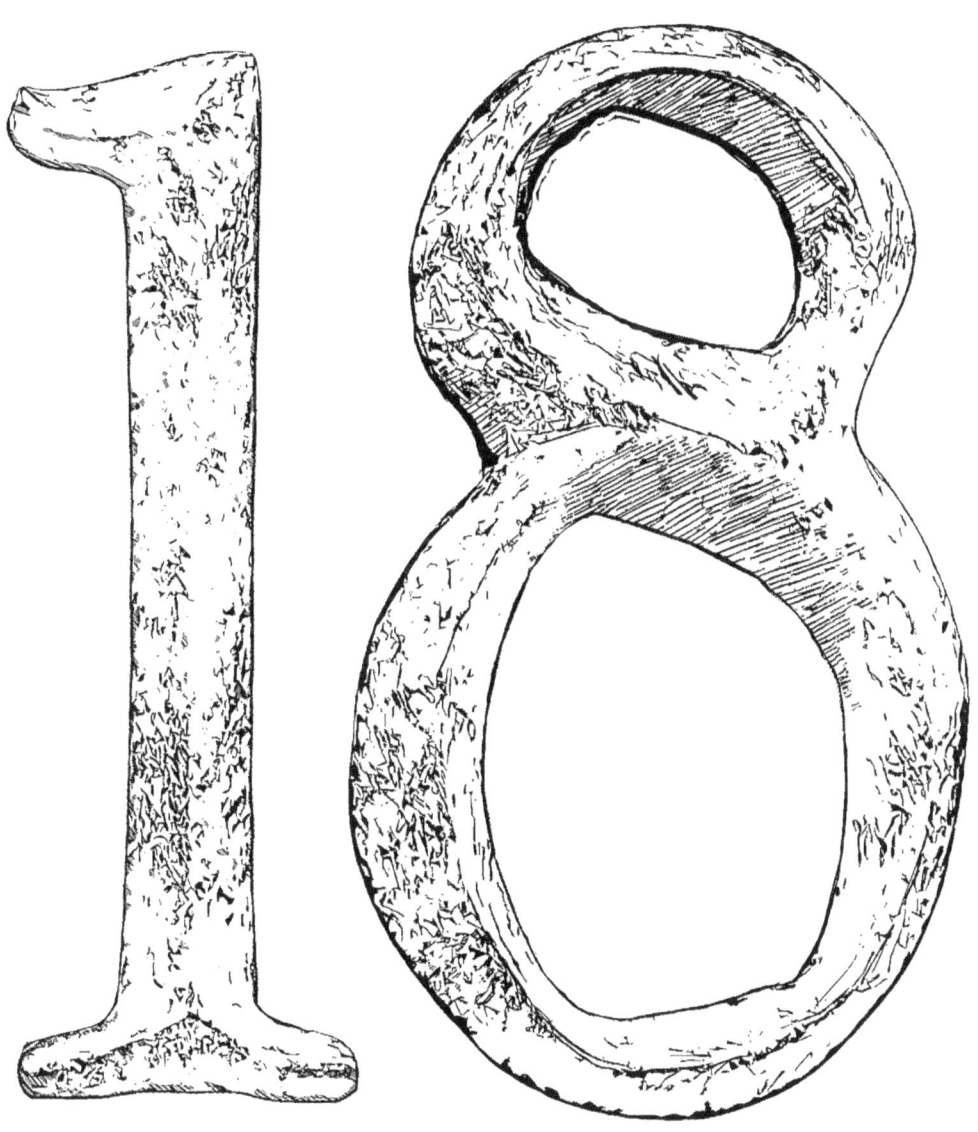

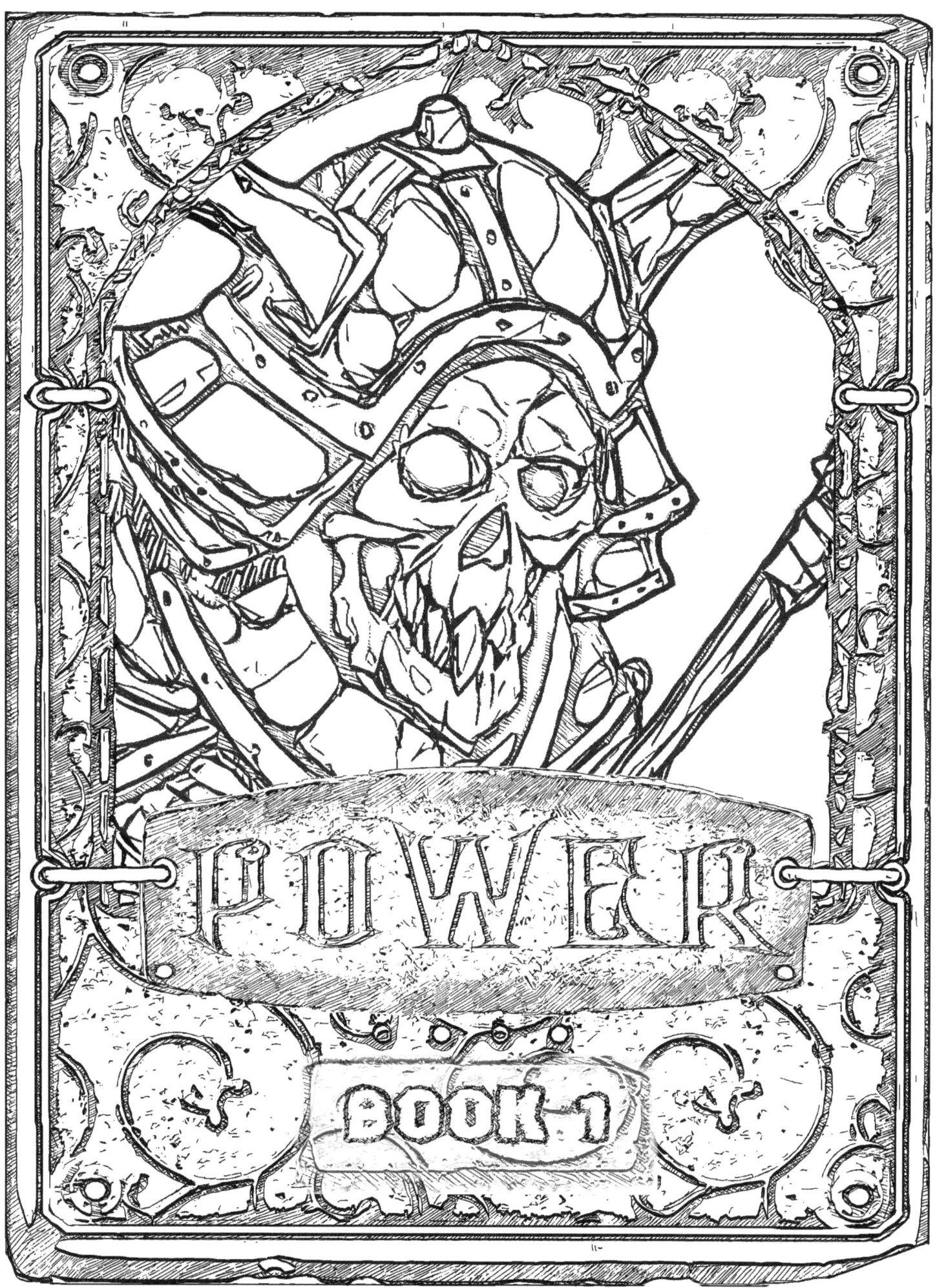

POWER

BOOK 1

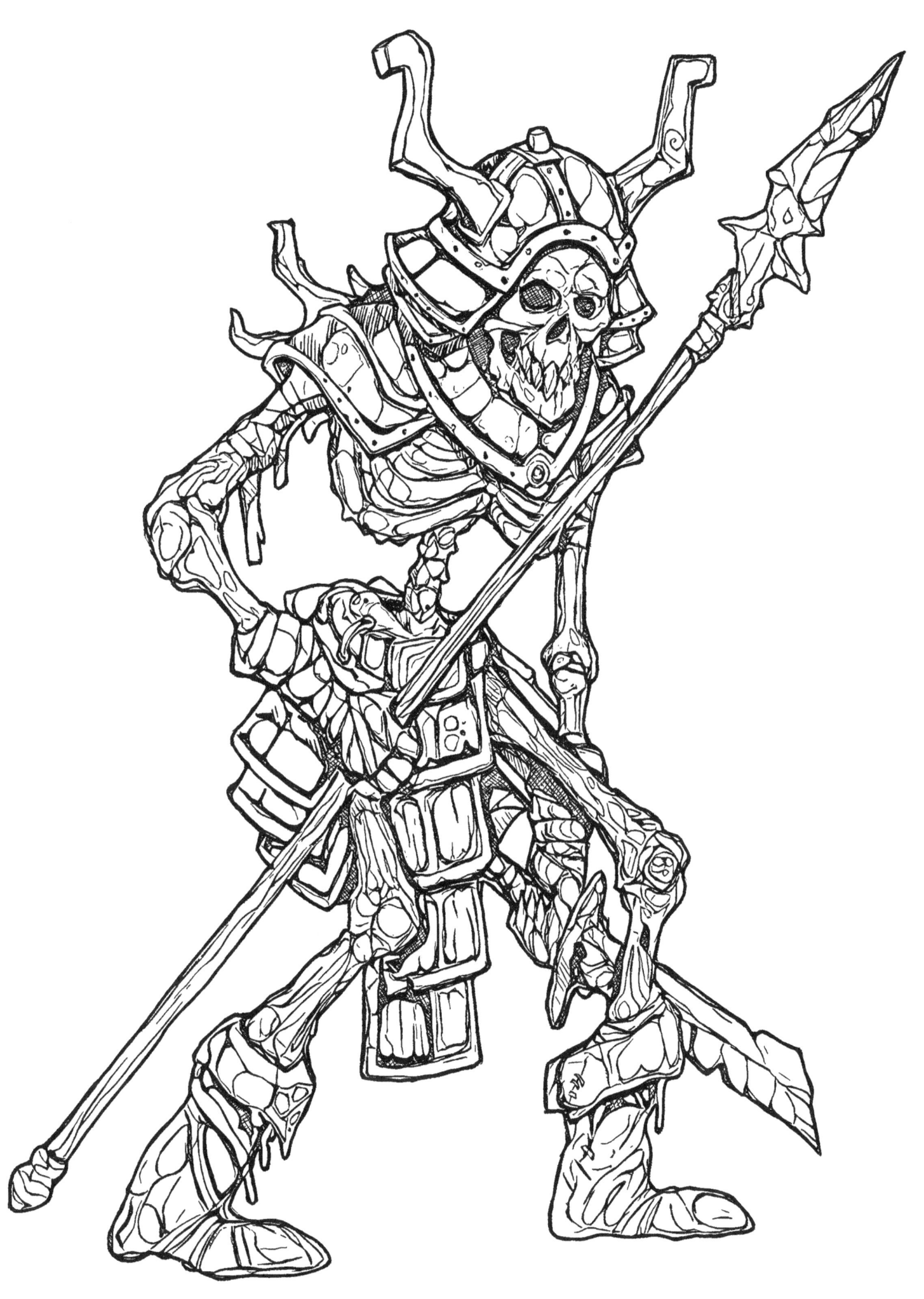

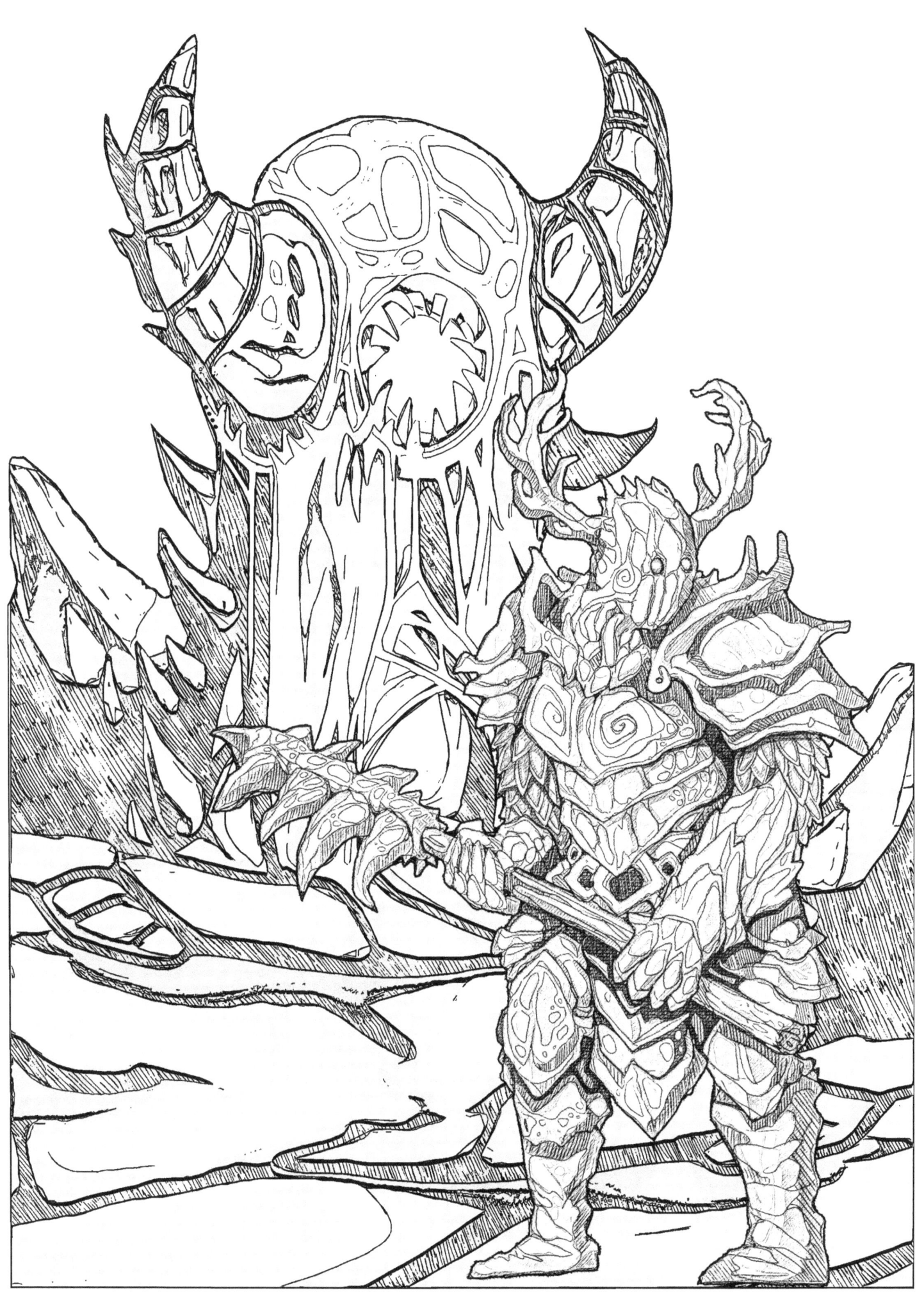

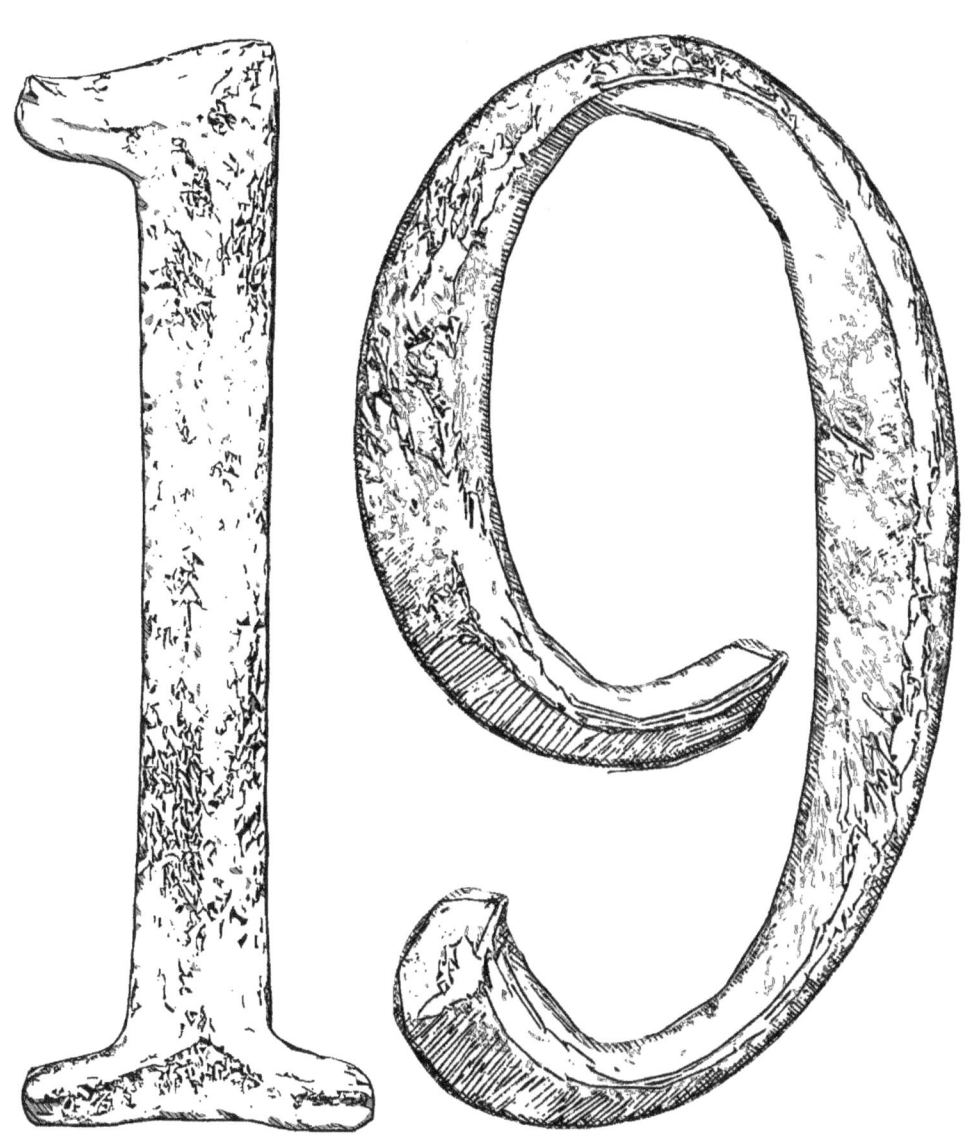

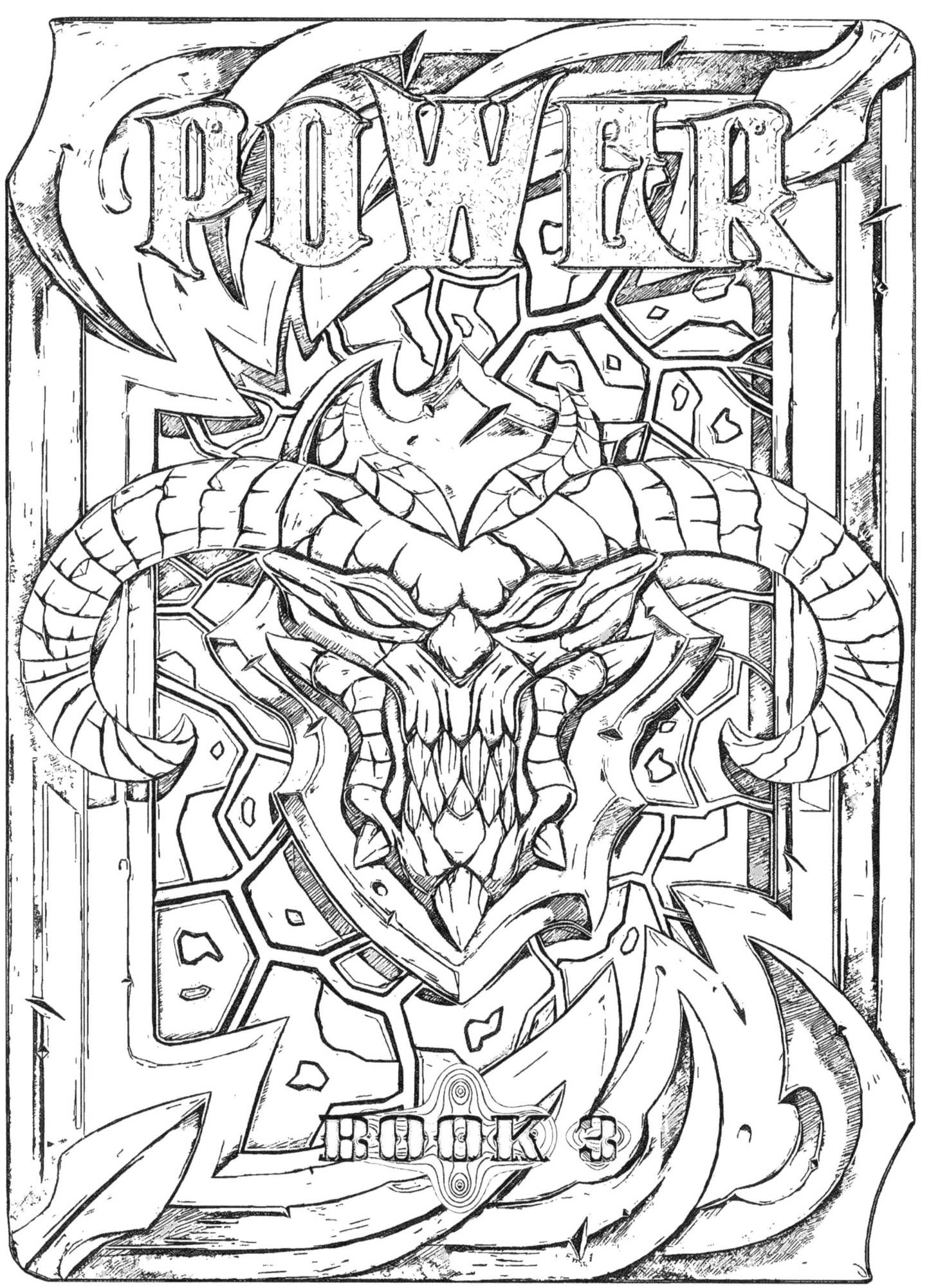

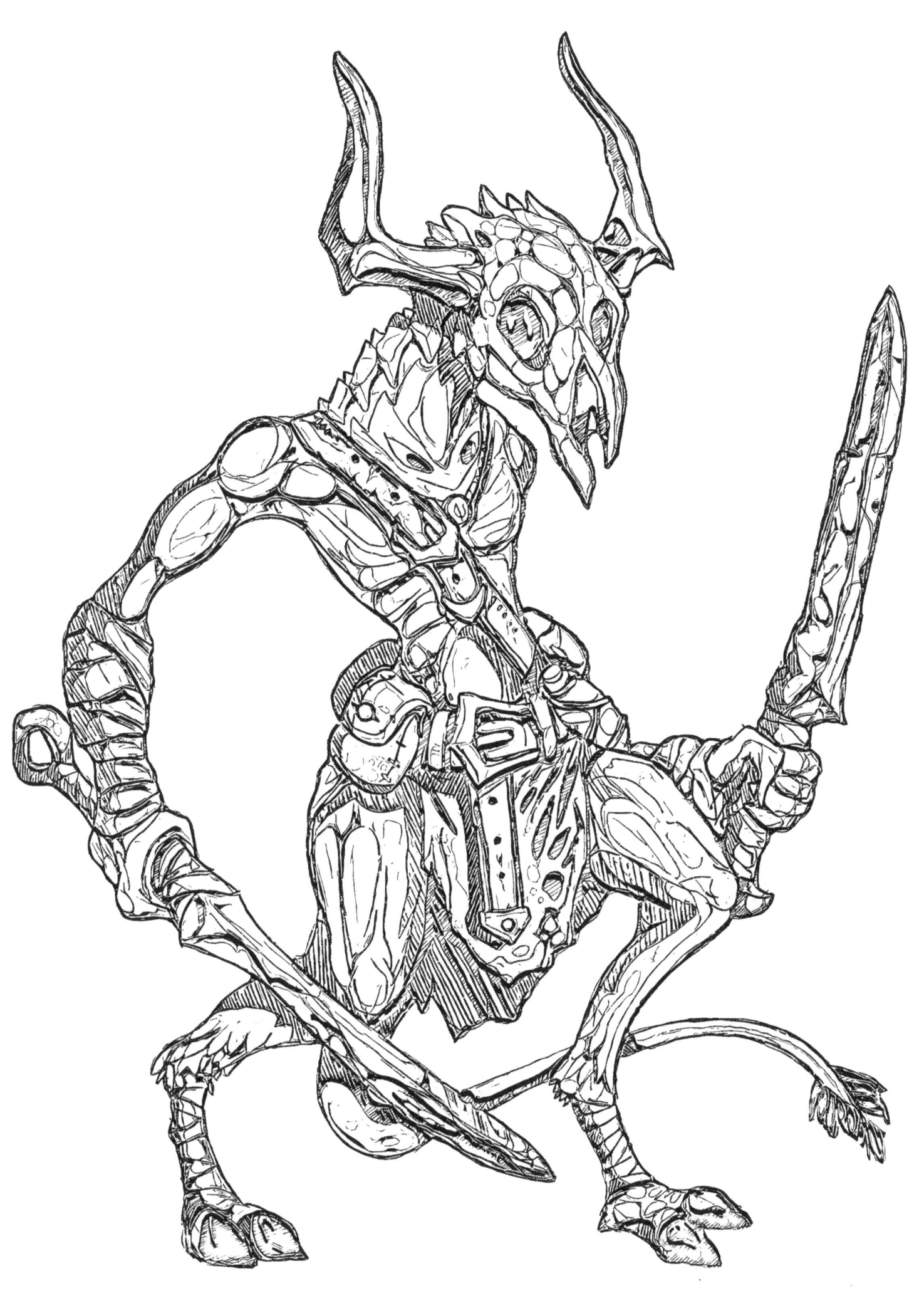

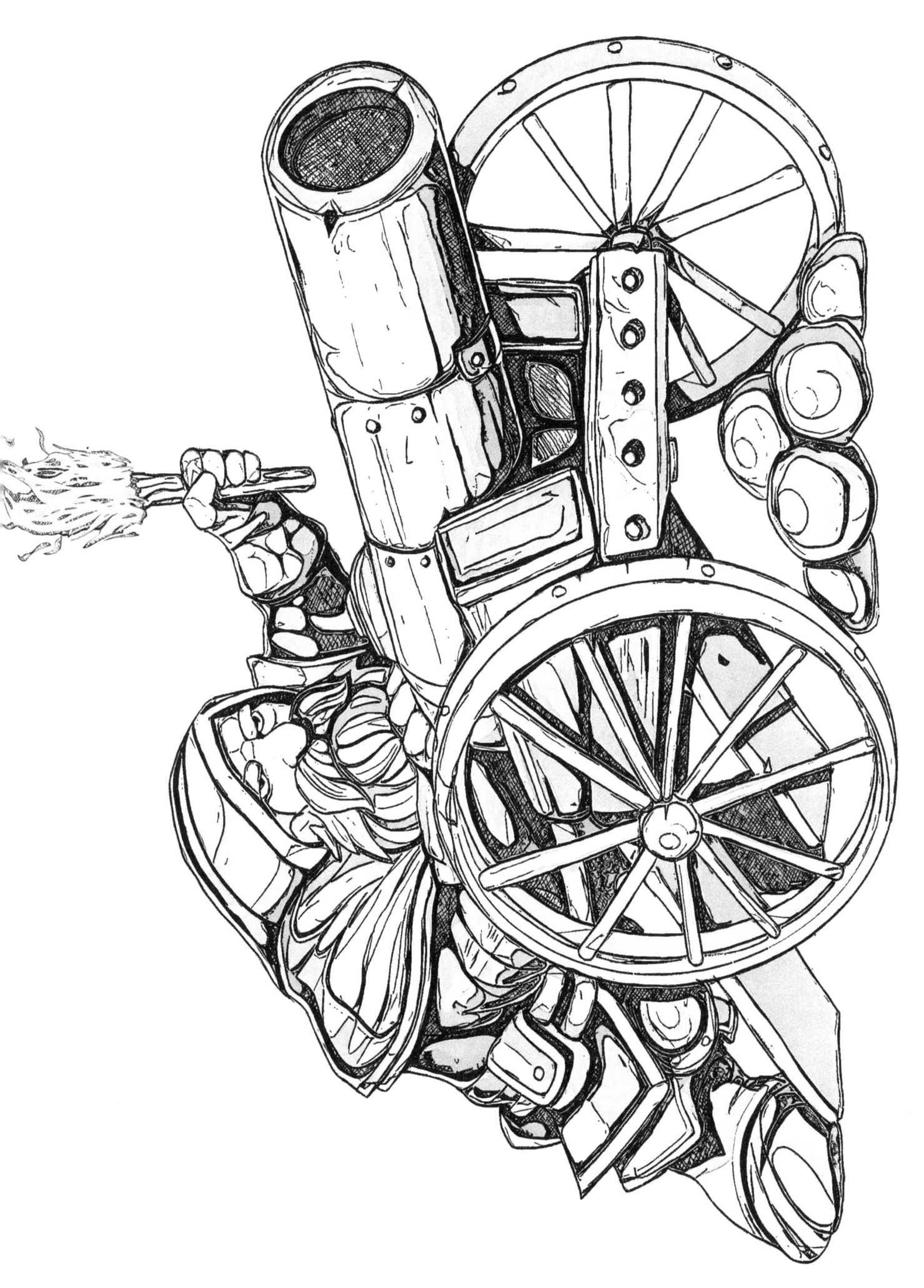

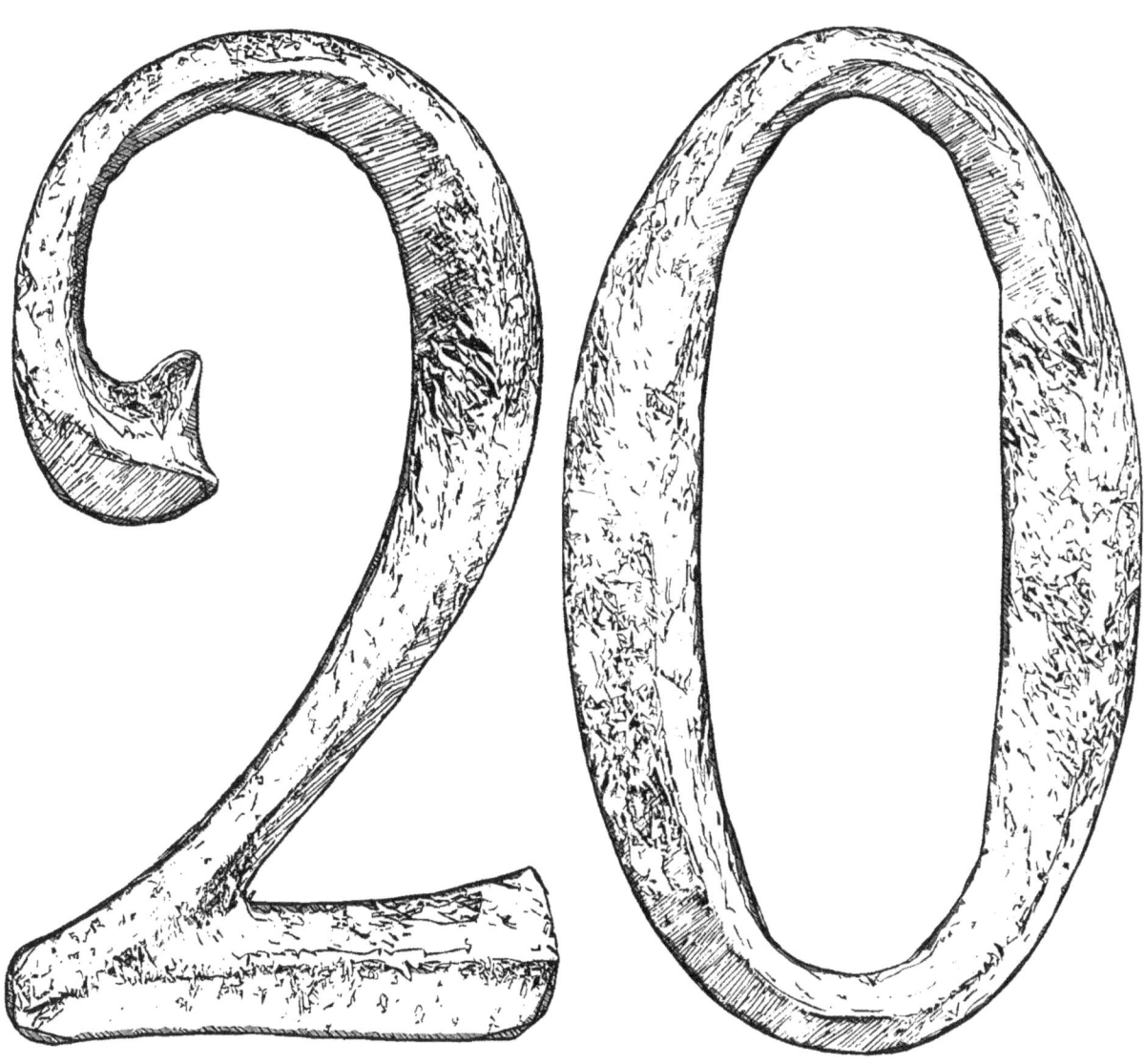

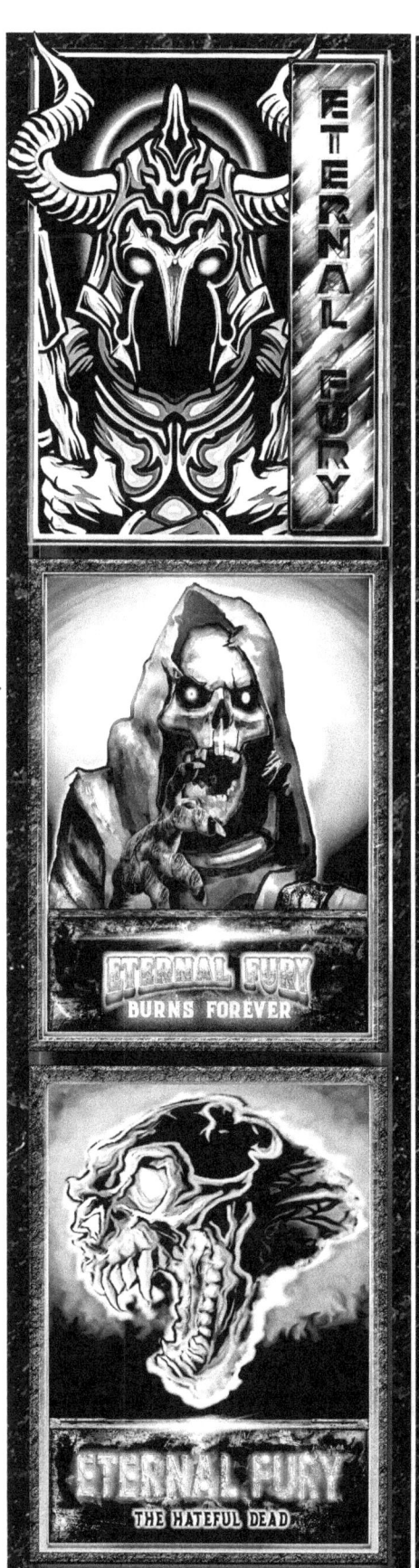

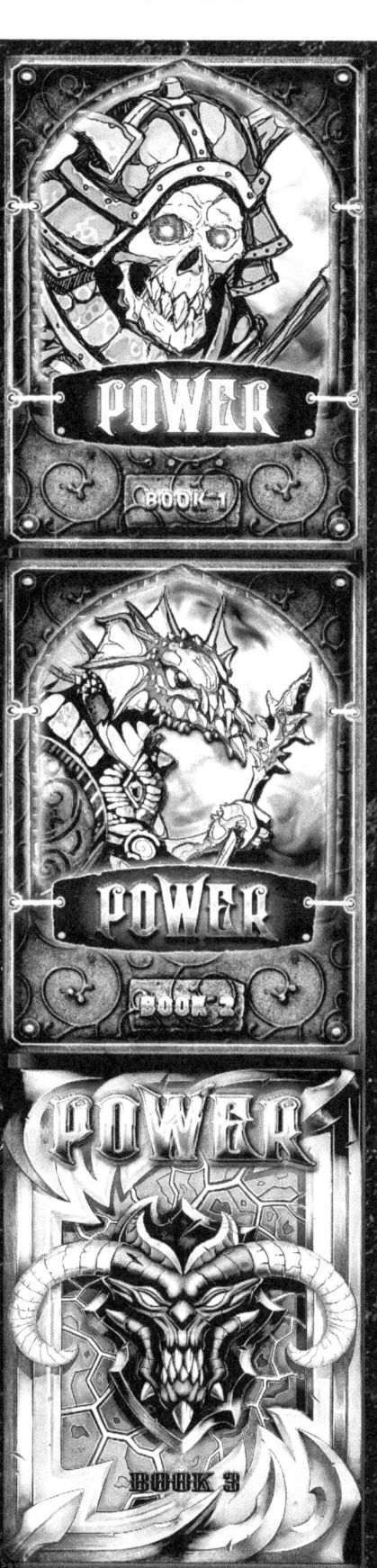

» COMBINES TWO BOOKS:

ETERNAL FURY

ETERNAL FURY: BURNS FOREVER

« COMBINES TWO BOOKS:

POWER: BOOK 1

POWER: BOOK 2